D1395744

'A compelling insigh   loves to
run for running's sak. . . . Connell is engaging when talking
about personal details . . . But it's his curiosity and enthusiasm
for all that's around him that makes this book truly connect
with the reader'   *Irish Independent*

'*The Running Book* takes the theme of running and opens it out
into something much wider. *The Cow Book* author has a style
that moves seamlessly across themes. Here, we get a history of
Longford, a personal journey and a reflection on the limits of
physical ability'   Niamh Donnelly, *Irish Times*

'A piece of work, ostensibly about running, which is so much
more and rewards the reader beyond an insight into one
discipline. This is a book rich in history, personal reflections
and questions regarding the limits of physical capability.
It is a book which can lead you to periods of self-reflection,
raises the impact of times gone by and weaves it together with
recollections of runs, challenges attempted and individuals
encountered'   *Culture*, RTÉ

'It quickly became obvious that not only was there a strong
theme of colonialism emerging from the historic landscape
that Connell was moving through, but also that here was a
book about happiness . . . In this difficult new world where a
walk or a run around the block might be the only respite your
mental health gets in a day of isolation, Connell's paean to the
activity couldn't be better timed'   *Sunday Independent*

'The author's speciality is the vignette. His book unfolds like
a series of 400-metre loops, circling around again and again
to the same place, although Connell's philosophical reflections
ripple ever wider in the process . . . Connell's wisdom is
grounded. Everything comes back to Longford, to the land,
and to Ireland's struggle for self-expression, which informs the
author's own'   Frank McNally, *Irish Times*

The Running Book

John Connell's work has been published in *Granta*'s 'New Irish Writing' issue. His memoir *The Cow Book* was a number one bestseller in Ireland and was *Ireland AM* Popular Non-Fiction Book of the Year at the 2018 An Post Irish Book Awards. He is a multi-award-winning investigative journalist and editor, film producer and playwright. He lives on his family farm, Birchview, in County Longford, Ireland.

The Running Book

A Journey through Memory, Landscape and History

JOHN CONNELL

PICADOR

First published 2020 by Picador

This paperback edition published 2021 by Picador
an imprint of Pan Macmillan
The Smithson, 6 Briset Street, London EC1M 5NR
EU representative: Macmillan Publishers Ireland Limited,
Mallard Lodge, Lansdowne Village, Dublin 4
Associated companies throughout the world
www.panmacmillan.com

ISBN 978-1-5290-4238-2

1 3 5 7 9 8 6 4 2

A CIP catalogue record for this book is available from the British Library.

Printed and bound by CPI Group (UK) Ltd, Croydon, CR0 4YY

For Stephen Rea
& Ross Laurence

Surely it is much more generous to forgive and remember, than to forgive and forget.

MARIA EDGEWORTH

The past is never dead. It's not even past.

WILLIAM FAULKNER

Prologue
Undiscovered lands

I've never run this far before. I'm thirty and this is all new to me. I'm running now as though everything depends on it and in so many ways it does. This run, this voyage, is in ways the climax of a journey into the country of the self. The final destination after a year of travelling.

I'm thinking of all this but really I'm just putting one foot in front of the other and willing myself on, hoping to keep going because I've quit at so many things in my life, ran away from problems and people, but right now this run is a way to make amends for all that. It might sound like magical thinking and maybe in some way it is. All actions start in dreams and thoughts and I've long held on to this one.

I'm in a local forest of Derrycassin in rural Longford, it has snowed and between the melting snow and puddles of water I race now. My feet are wet but I do not mind. My lungs are strong and firm and I know and feel that at this pace I can continue for a long time, an hour more, two hours more I am not sure.

This is an undiscovered country.

A man once said to me you get to know yourself on a long run. In the end, he surmised, you realise you're a lot stronger than you think and a lot more stubborn. Those words are haunting me now. They are every one of them true.

Running and farming are two things I understand, two tangible things. With each passing day progress is made. The cultivation of a crop or cow is like the tending of the garden of the self; not much happens in a week, but in the culmination of weeks and months real progress is made, real goals achieved. Everything starts in dreams and thoughts, the building of a farm, the building of a body, the writing of a book. We are, I think, in a way, the heirs of our dreams.

The sweat on my face has dried and turned to salt and when I lick my lips I can taste it. It has been several hours since I have drank water: at times a craving comes to me for it and then like a lustful urge it leaves again. I tell myself that soon, soon I will stop and give in. There is a river and lake beside me, beside this old forest: perhaps when all this is over I will jump in, quench and cool myself. I'll cup my hands and drink the water from the lake fresh and clean like the old people did in the long ago.

I am not the greatest runner but I have in me the discipline of an athlete. Running and exercise have given me a control of my life, a real foundation on which to build, and from that the new man that I have become has been forged.

They say running is a lonely thing but out there on the road, on the roads of life, I have never felt more alive, more connected to the moment.

In the forest, the path winds and courses through steep hills and bends, I have names for some of them, secret silly names to help me surmount and overcome them. The gravel is loose underneath my feet as I beat out my weary rhythm. I am alone here today, there is only the forest, the lake and me.

At Switzerland bend I feel the glee of the flat ground return. The huge pine trees surround me and I imagine myself in some Scandinavian place, some Valhalla of nature, some distant land. I hear the lake waters lap and fold onto themselves. I know that soon the hills of the forest will be upon me and I will have to strain and push myself forward.

I have been running for twenty-five kilometres now and with each passing lap I urge myself forward.

There are jobs to be done at home, cattle that need to be cleaned out, feed to be given. My phone does not work here and while I run in this place I am not contactable. I like it that way. It is just the road and me.

My headphones beat out a steady rhythm of 70s pop and easy rock music that keeps me happy and motivated. Alone here now I shout out the words of Blue Swede's 'Hooked on a Feeling'. There was a time I couldn't sing any more, that I had not the joy of life; but these words, as my actions now do too, remind me that there is so much joy in the world, joy amidst the darkness.

The snows have turned to slush as I round the corner and hit the thirty kilometres mark. I am hot and remove my jumper, throwing it on top of a nearby bush.

I must be careful now to ensure I do not catch a cold when I finish. The day is cold but I am hot and alive and I think now of all those who run with me, of the ancients, of Murakami, of the Olympians.

When I was a boy I loved to run but as a student I put that aside thinking the life of the mind to be an immobile one. In the last two years, after everything, I have come to see that the intellectual life, as Seneca said, is interlinked, that true happiness is found in the present moment and that physical labour and thought are the same. My feet are the extension of my thoughts and it is intellectual will that gets me around this course, not just mere physical fitness.

At thirty-four kilometres I hit the wall. I am in the land of the new, the place beyond the pines. I have never run this far before but I have the will in me to continue.

I have every will but my body is beginning to tire.

My foot pains have returned, I can feel a build-up of lactic acid in my shoulder and my calf muscle is beginning to ache. I run on for another kilometre ignoring my failing engine.

I do not know the rules of this country, its customs; perhaps in the land of thirty-five kilometres there is only pain and ignorance. Perhaps it is a corroboree of effort and sweat culminating in the discovery of the dreamtime of the self. In my mind I think of all the places I have been, all the journeys I have undertaken.

This run is a part of that story. I will remember it in the list of great days I have had on this earth.

A man gets to know himself on the road and in me I have

found a multitude of histories; a conflict of nations, of language, of faith.

In the recess of the past I see my grandfather on the run, fighting in the War of Independence in his flying column, moving from safe house to safe house. It was only weeks ago that my father told me that he had been captured and imprisoned in that time. What would he make of me now? His namesake, running in a forest for no other reason than life itself.

By the water's lapping edge I imagine the older people, too, the Celts who once ruled this place. They are all of them in me and I in them.

A landlord once owned all this, this lake, this forest. I am running on colonised land. Running as a post-colonial man, whatever that is.

I think now I must be getting delirious and perhaps I am.

'*Murderalise 'em, Rock!*' I shout out aloud now, uttering my old *Rocky* movie mantra to snap me back into the present.

My feet are tired, my body sore and the Italian stallion urges me on in my mind, asking for just one more step.

At the last turn I near the end of my race. It has been four hours or more. I carry my wounded body across my imaginary line. There are no waiting crowds, no cheering lover, no landlords or IRA men. It is just me and the forest and the cold winter's day in rural Ireland.

I slow to a walk, stumbling towards the grass of nearby Mullinalaghta Gaelic football field. I hunker down to catch my breath. I am thirty, I have never run this far, I have never felt so alive.

Running through time

When I look around the farms of our neighbours they form a landscape. A cumulative thing, that we call Soran, our home.

The landscape is Irish, or to the outsider it would seem that way, and yet when I think now it is a landscape formed of history. A living palette of the colonial.

The fields which I work are a Norman creation, the hedgerows containing their beech and oak an English lord's fancy. The living landscape in this place is in a sense ruled by the dead.

What is history, I wonder now as I trundle around the farmyard making my way to visit our sheep. A learned phenomenon? This mind of mine is a reflector of all the landscape says and all that I know of it.

If the books of the past were torn down and our memories of this place removed, what then would it be? Would I know it only as the sheep do? For its folds and bends, its rivers and ditches. And yet the sheep too have memory. They know where to go for shelter each year, where the best grass is.

Perhaps a place removed of memory is what the early settlers felt when they usurped the Native Americans' land, a place bereft of story, so they thought, and yet was it not rich with it?

What does such a place feel like? I do not know because

we Irish cannot forget as much as our old master cannot remember. There is the history of the place as wrote and the history of the place as recalled but they are both so different, so at odds.

It was in this way of thinking that I began a run through my home county of Longford.

The cows on the farm have been put out to grass, the long winter months are over and the death-dishevelled earth has come alive once more. Between the moving out and the harvest of the meadow grounds life has become quieter, easier. It's a nice time on a farm. A time when a man has room to think of big things.

I ran through home. Why? Because I was fit enough, I suppose, but also to understand this place more. In the running I came too to remember other great runs and runners; they move like ghosts through the landscape too, but also personal ones that I carry with me as memories and inspiration.

I ran through the artefact of my county, through its roads and villages, through the landscape shaped by a thousand yesterdays and a thousand more tomorrows.

Free running

The day is fine, the weather good. I pull on my running tights and shorts, a baseball hat and a light jumper. I have a few little energy gel packets to bring with me and a small bag of nuts. I pack lightly, I will drink water on the move; there are some small rivers and lakes where I can pause and if I can't reach them I bring some cash just in case.

Preparation is essential in running long distances. We all have our little rituals, a favourite T-shirt, a playlist of music. No two runners are the same. I'm not, I know, one of the hard-core runners. I don't own a sports watch or a distance counter. I run not to break records; for me it's enough just to be out on the road with a good song and the country passing by.

I wasn't always great for stretching, but after nearly a year of repeated injuries and our local physiotherapist scolding me on every visit I've gotten into the habit. I bend and stretch, pull and flex, my muscles know now what is coming and I must say there's a certain joy in being able to touch one's toes again, something childlike and innocent in the enjoyment of being limber.

I begin as I have begun so many times before, down our short lane onto the main road. Veering left I start.

Lacing up

In my childhood bedroom there's an old drawer full of sports day trophies. They are by and large for athletics of one form or another. I was never any good at team sports, being a bit clumsy when the pressure was on, and it seemed running, even then, suited my temperament.

I hold their small frames now. Running them through my hands they shine still. I do not know how they ended up in this drawer, perhaps my mother put them there as a reminder of the little boy I was whilst I was away being a wild colonial boy.

Things come into one's life again at strange times, at times when we need them. I have heard it called objective chance.

As a writer they so often come to me in the form of books or phrases which, at a time of writing, guide me, lead me on further towards the ultimate goal of finishing a work, teaching me in some new way.

These things at another time would mean nothing, would be insensible, but when the antenna of the self is switched on they can mean everything, changing, as my friend Father Sean calls it, the uncertain world of reality into a certain one if only for the briefest moment.

The trophies hold their weight and memory in my hands. I don't think I've lifted them in twenty years. It is a nice reminder of the innocence of youth and the wonder of movement.

Déjà vu

On the face of it, I get up, I put on my runners and I go out the door and run. On the face of it, so often a man runs in a circle, ending up where he started, having achieved, to the outsider, nothing; only to make himself tired, sweaty and oftentimes exhausted.

I used to think runners were actors in a perpetual déjà vu. Now, however, I see that each time is a new journey, a new experience.

No run is ever the same; a man can run the same track every day and, like a river, find it is always different. It's not the track that changes, it's us.

The genius of life, I've come to see, is that what I have felt out there on the road is the same as what Linford Christie felt when he ran. What I have thought is no different to what the philosophers have thought. That which connects us, our humanity, makes it as a bridge to every other human.

When I take the bend for home mid-run, my body drenched in sweat, my heartbeat elevated, I'm as close to Usain Bolt as I'll ever be.

You never run alone when you race. It is never a déjà vu.

Longford

Longford is my home. It is neither a big nor a very famous place. It's situated in the heart of the Irish midlands, right in the middle of the country; it is not a tourist destination, we have no great peaks or mountain ranges, and yet there is a beauty here in the rolling drumlin grounds, in the bogs that surround us and hold our memories, and in the lakes that litter our landscape and the people who journey through it.

Our history on this island does not start in Rome or Athens, it begins in quiet places such as this.

It was once the very edge of Empire, a frontier town on the fringe of the then Elizabethan world. This was as far as civilisation went, beyond which lay the wilds of the Western men, where the Gael still ruled and law and order were of a different kind.

By the seventeenth century, with the crushing of the last native uprisings the county was divided and planted by English and Scottish settlers and so began the first great experiments of the English Empire: colonisation.

Longford, though small, has again and again played a role in the future of the nation. From rebellions to politicians, it has been as a small vanguard.

I start from the end of the lane. The wildflowers and weeds are growing along the ditches, everywhere is a riot of green. The wildflowers are beautiful things and appear as gems along the roadside, calling all life to them. It is my hope to plant the land with these flowers in the next few weeks to help the bees and so repay some of our exchequer with nature.

I check my pace and move forward, slow and steady.

I am in the land of the Connells. We live at the edge of our own small empire, the last few homes on the outskirts of the townland of Soran in the parish of Killoe. My uncle and two aunts live beside us with their families. We form an enclave and the older men joke that we Soran folk are like one of the wandering tribes of the Bible, for we are Killoe people but go to mass in the nearby village and next parish of Ballinalee but are buried in Killoe. We belong, it seems, to neither tribe and it suits us that way.

Soran has changed since my childhood; it had its own characters then, mostly bachelors but some women too, who were in a way the bards of the area, the keepers of the folk memories.

My grandmother Mary was one of the last of them. As I pass her lane, the last home in the area, I think of her. We had many great times together and I learned as much as I could of her knowledge, but one cannot absorb ninety-two years of living into the mind of a young man.

Her illness was swift and painless, it was what she had always wanted; a good quick death. She died at home in her own bed and we are glad of that. It was a death of the *sean nós*, the old way, and our centuries-old tradition of wakes served us well. The ritual, I see now, is not for the dead but the living.

We still talk of her nearly a year after her passing, thinking that she might return for a mug of tea and a good chat on a fair day. Close to her end, as my mother and aunts nursed her, she spoke of something that has stayed with us:

'Life is given to you; you do not choose it. Life is to be lived and enjoyed.'

I run now with those words in my heart, for she above others knew this well.

Writing and running

Writing and running are not such strange bedfellows. They are both slow and gradual, both based on discipline and routine. One must show up to the great event, be it a laptop or a road trial. One must put in the hard yards.

I've been running seriously for a few years and by serious I mean that running a half-marathon is not hard. Running has become part of my life and changed how I see things. It has, in some ways too, I think, changed how I write.

It wasn't some Pauline moment, some Damascene event; rather it was the culmination of a thousand moments, a thousand breaths out there on the road, one foot moving simply in front of the other, where I found a long-missing part of myself.

Dr George Sheehan, a philosopher of the running movement, called it being a good animal; that man is at his heart an animal of movement, for why else do we have such long legs.

It began as a want for change. I had emerged from a serious illness and the idea of fitness, of building a new me, came upon me in the way I have heard musicians talk of songs descending from above. Running was to become a foundation block in the cultivation of the garden of the self.

I think a great deal when I am out running, whole passages of stories and books come to me, filling me with new ways of seeing. When I am stuck for material, the road, that seemingly empty place, is full and rich with ideas.

Murakami, the great Japanese writer, has of course illuminated the path before me. Sometimes in my daydreams I imagine him and me running together through some forest. He is smaller than me but his body is lithe and strong. We run in silence, tackling hills and valleys, one not wanting to submit to the other. I the novice and he the master.

I imagine myself holding firm, going toe to toe with the

great man. Afterwards we share a bottle of cold water and then he nods and says you're OK kid and runs off.

My friend Matt is a therapist and recently he told me of his studies into the analysis of dreams. They are in many ways our playing out of scenarios. In our dreams life can be righted, mistakes mended, and ultimately peace that was denied in reality can be found in this world.

Murakami and I will never run together but he has taught me a great deal, through running, about being a writer.

Comanche dead

Leaving behind my homeland of Soran I move across the Camlin river to Ballinalee. I am in Comanche country now, the land of our rivals. Situated atop a crossroads, this is as close as we come to an outpost in rural Ireland. It was once a land of outlaws and bandits. It has known blood and despair, death and war.

There are few villages like it, few places with such providence in blood.

I move up the slow hill to the crossroads. It is a small place of only a few hundred people and yet its inhabitants have changed the world.

In 1798 Irish intellectuals began a revolution of the mind. Inspired by the rising of the free French (who would go on to help them), the rebellion was to unite Ireland's native Catholics and planted Protestants to rise up and seize control of their own destiny and wrest it from the hands of Britain. It was a defining moment in the history of this land and a time that is talked of still, some two hundred-odd years later.

The rebellion of the United Irishmen, led by Theobald Wolfe Tone, a northern Presbyterian, ended here in Longford at the Battle of Ballinamuck just a few short miles from my home. That rebellion was to captivate my young mind, for the bicentenary of the events occurred when I was a young boy in school and for that year of 1998 our principal, Master Harte, weaved the story of the men's rising and of their fall. History, he said, was all around us, shaping us, and we did not need to look overseas to find our own home-grown heroes.

General Humbert

Those rising men of Longford were led by the French general Humbert, who had arrived weeks before in the country's west. His aim: to reignite the revolutionary zeal and free Ireland.

Humbert was lucky at first and after disembarking in Killala, on 23 August 1798, won the Battle of Castlebar. Though he was outnumbered, the battle has long been remembered for the resounding defeat of the British, leading to their routing.

On his landing, Humbert had declared the formation of the Republic of Connaught, which was to replace the Kingdom of Ireland. Speaking from his landing ground, he said:

Liberty, Equality, Fraternity, Union!
After several unsuccessful attempts, behold at last
Frenchmen arrived amongst you . . . Union, Liberty, the
Irish Republic! Such is our shout. Let us march. Our
hearts are devoted to you; our glory is in your happiness.

The Republic was in real terms a quasi-state, with no actual power other than pressing Irish men to join the French and fight. Perhaps it may have grown into something but it was never given the time. It would fall just weeks later on the 8th of September.

To my left lies Bully's Acre. It is but a small green field nestled beside our church and playground. It was here that the Republic of Connaught and its ideals ended. It was here that Cornwallis enacted his final victory.

The Battle of Ballinamuck was doomed to failure. Humbert, commanding a force of just 2,500, was surrounded by 15,000 troops under Cornwallis's command on his right and 14,000 men under General Lake behind. After a short action of no more than half an hour, Humbert surrendered.

Ninety-six French and 748 Irish men were taken prisoner. They were marched from Ballinamuck across our very fields, as my father reminds me still, to this place, to our village. The men were hanged in trees (which stood until recently when a neighbour and family friend cut them down for pain of the memory) and buried in quicklime. The lime burned and rotted their skin, a final insult over the defeated dead, making so as never to be able to reinter them.

Master Harte told us school children then that we should be proud not that they died but that they rose.

Humbert himself was not executed and was instead repatriated and returned to France. He would later fight in the Caribbean and fall in love with Napoleon's sister Pauline, herself a married woman. His was to be a life of action and adventure.

I wipe the small beads of sweat from my brow as I think of the dead. We have no great memorial to them here but we do not forget what is buried beneath us.

Papa Francesco

The world has a new Pope. I ran with him one night.

I have long wanted to make a pilgrimage to the Holy City

of Rome to say simply thank you to God for helping me get through everything, for helping me become a writer.

I had visions of this place, of walking through the Vatican feeling its awe and splendour, strolling along the Tiber, drinking espresso and generally being a romantic Italian.

The trip with my girlfriend Vivian was supposed to be a joyous thing, but instead it turned into a source of fighting and rows as the business and stress of the city got to us. That was until Il Papa and I met.

Good Friday is a most sacred day for Christians, a high holiday of Easter when the passion of Christ occurred. It is the day of his death, the day when no Eucharist is given, a day when we reflect as a people.

It was late in the evening when I set out to run. The evening lights of the city grew bright and a warmth and smell of jasmine filled the air. I ran through the back streets of the inner-city district of Monti, moving past cafes and restaurants following some vague direction south. At the Parco di Colle Oppio, I spat and felt the adrenaline rush through my veins. It seemed to me like the Garden of Gethsemane, beautiful and Mediterranean with its columns and stone pines. Moving down the park's hill I emerged to the lit-up Colosseum and the sight of thousands of people.

The roads around this ancient battleground were closed to vehicles and so I ran along them unfettered and unmolested.

A huge illuminated cross emanated from atop the ruins of

the Palatine Hill as TV cameras and hundreds of army and policemen looked on.

Il Papa, Pope Francis, was inside praying the stations of the cross, moving through prayer by prayer of the passion of the Christ as we have been taught.

As I stepped now so did he and we strolled together around the Colosseum, he within and I without, in a communion of movement.

I blessed myself as I heard his words, in some way to let him know that I was there, that I was a witness too.

As I neared the Arch of Constantine, the very place where Roman emperors entered the city in triumph, I broke away, turning left and down the empty road towards the Circus Maximus. The words of Francis echoed through the streets.

Italian soldiers and priests standing side by side nodded to me as I beat out my worn rhythm, a lone figure running away from the waiting crowds.

The Circus Maximus was the largest stadium in ancient Rome, home to chariot racing and games; it is now a public park for all to use. Where once 150,000 spectators watched sporting greats I took a gravel-worn track and began my circuit.

I was alone there that Easter night, in the place where men must have prayed to the old gods for help and victory in the long ago. In a place where dreams began and ended. At the final bend I heard the words of the Pope ring out and thousands answer: Amen. In this, the city where the idea of Empire began, where the idea of slave and master took root, where the old gods meet the new.

I turned for home, both a traveller through history and a pilgrim of faith. The words of Il Papa floating around me, running beside me.

From Ballinalee to Byron Bay

I turn right at Bully's Acre and remark on the fact that the famous general Cornwallis himself stayed here for three days after the defeat of the rebel Irish and French forces in 1798.

Cornwallis' arrival would have been something of a stir in the village (then called St. Johnstown), for here was the man who had effectively lost the American colonies in the US War of Independence after his surrender at the siege of Yorktown in 1781. He had met Washington and also been denied the honour of marching his defeated troops out of battle by the man. And yet he was not a maligned figure. Both a knight and the former Governor-General of India from 1786 to 1794, he had helped expand the Empire's spread there with the help of the East India Company.

His defeat then, of the Irish in 1798, had come at a time when the British were grappling with the problem of keeping their empire together. It is perhaps why he had dealt so cruelly with the dissenting men of Ballinamuck.

At the hill of the village I run past our neighbours, the

Forster's, house. The Forster's have been stalwarts of the village for hundreds of years and friends of the family for just as long.

The matriarch of the family, Rose, was a dear friend, an elderly woman who I came to know through my regular visits to the house where the village mill once resided by the Camlin river. Rose, by virtue of her age, became the font of the Anglo-Irish history of the area, and her door was a beaten track with long-departed families looking for their ancestors.

On one such visit she showed me pictures of the village just before World War One. In them were contained the faces of the ancient forebears of all our neighbours. The village has changed greatly and yet in some ways has retained its ancient magical powers.

As I run by the Protestant graveyard I think of Tommy, Rose's son who passed away just a few months ago. Tommy was a part of our lives since childhood. A talented farmer and storyteller, he often regaled me with the tales of his deep family history, such as his great great uncle Thomas who became an army surgeon in the Napoleonic wars and whose son William went on to be the Governor of New South Wales in Australia.

William was a man of action who married the daughter of Gregory Blaxland the explorer, who was the first European to cross the Blue Mountains of Australia, opening up the grasslands of the interior to cattle and sheep grazing. In 1840, ever the explorer, William and Gregory teamed up to lead herds of sheep into the Clarence valley. By the end of that decade William owned some 64,000 acres of farmland.

'William did well,' Tommy told me once as I researched his famous relation to understand what the early days of Australia were like. Indeed, in the years to come I would travel through towns and regions named after him throughout Australia. Not bad for a son of the native soil.

Tommy and his wife Frances have for decades now loaned their lands for the local Connemara pony show, and so in thinking of Tommy I think of all those long, hot summers where we walked through the village as part of the parade, and where in Tommy's fields we watched the riders and horses surmount the jumps and fences of the eventing course.

It was here that our old horse Hazel won best foal and buyers came from all around to purchase her, but my mother, ever the lover of horses, said she would stay with us and breed another winner.

Tommy had a deep liking for shorthorn cattle and his herd boasted some of the best breeding in the area.

Tommy's passing has left a vacancy in our hearts that will never truly be healed. At his funeral we lined the streets of the village with the local football club, the Connemara society and hundreds of other mourners to pay our last respects to him.

In the church there was no room to sit or stand, so great was his liking that the crowds stood in the freezing cold.

My father has told me he has visited his grave many times

since his passing to tell him of the local news and to check that he is happy.

So often in history we remember the great men but forget the everyday heroes. Tommy was one of them and for that he will never die.

Chasing waterfalls

Passing by the Forsters' house I reach the brow of the hill. In the distance, on Lough Gurteen, swans and waterfowl play.

A neighbour passes by, waving to me. They have grown used to me running the roads now, beating my path along the tarmac. They do not ask me why I run.

It occurs to me that there are two types of runners: those who run for something and those who run from something.

The *for*s are easy enough to spot, they move along in aid of a charity, in aid of a smaller dress size for the big day, in aid of a new life balance.

But the others, the ones who run *from* something, they are a darker breed, a harder, more unknowable race.

They run from failed relationships, from the torment of drink or drugs. They give everything to the moment, seizing the now in the hope of making up for misspent yesterdays.

We are all of us in this together, we are all of us chasing something. The ghost of a personal best, the want for a better body, the vow never to fall again.

★

We all run to something. One of my best runs was for a steak.

Perhaps it is this cloud of colonial Australia but the run has come back to me now.

It was summer and I was in the Blue Mountains of New South Wales. I was writing my first book and my friend Bob came to visit me.

Bob is not quite like anyone else I know, a small man with a big personality; a businessman, builder, painter, a dead ringer for Andre Agassi. There's not much he can't put his hand to (he's built a boat with his bare hands). He has been an unfailing friend for a long time. He even hosted my first book launch at his cinema.

The Blue Mountains are an ancient and wonderful place, dense and green, full of nature and life. The day was hot when we set out, our hats upon our heads, down the steep roads from my writing cabin to the national park below.

Through streets and bush tracks we moved and ran, Bob, then I, leading the way.

'This is bloody great, mate,' he shouted to me as the sunlight passed through the trees and made gods of us in the midday sun.

A chorus of Australian birdsong rang in our ears in their ancient barking way and it was the voice of an entire world.

We twisted and moved, descending lower and lower until we reached the Park entrance, then began to jog down step after step, taking in gorges and cliff faces. I stumbled but Bob led us on; he had been here before, he knew the way.

We ran through the forest as the ancient Aboriginal warriors Pemulwuy and Windradyne might have done in the long ago. South-east of the mountains lies the region of Appin and it was here that one of the worst massacres of Australian colonial history happened. The massacre saw fourteen Dharawal people forced off a cliff and fall to their deaths. The colonial troops then decapitated the men and shipped their heads back to England. It was said at the time by many settlers that murder was a necessity of colonization. The colonization of Australia, particularly eastern Australia, was carried out as intermittent wars, raids and massacres. For many resistance fighters, their names would never be remembered, and perhaps worse, their fights for freedom were denigrated by being recorded by the occupying British as simply 'inhospitable meetings'.

Aboriginal people say the land where massacres occurred feels different. I have been to some of these places: they are changed lands that have lost a part of themselves that will never be recovered.

Appin is a fact I know all too well, for it was my Aboriginal friend Tess who told me of it during my stays with her on hot summer nights in Sydney. As the saying goes: white Australia has a black history.

As Bob and I ran on, the ghost of the past behind us, we saw what we had been chasing: the longed-for Wentworth waterfall.

'This is where Darwin came, mate,' Bob shouted, knowing that I love history.

'Who – Charles Darwin?' I replied, now shouting louder over the thundering noise of the rapids.

'I don't know another bloody one,' he replied.

It was here, in this place, that the great scientist cemented his beliefs on evolution, they say. Seeing the birds, the trees, everything in its place as alien to his eyes and yet beautifully the same and adapted.

We stopped at the waterfall and watched the water pour and pound the ancient red rock. The falling mist cooled our skin for we had run for a half-hour or more. The mosquitos were not so fierce here and did not bite us.

On the way back up the now-gruelling hills Bob suggested that working men need a good piece of meat, something for them to run towards.

As the sweat returned and the dryness of the Australian day hit us, we kept time with the image of that steak in our minds.

'We'll have to have a nice glass of wine with it,' I said.

'And a few chips,' Bob returned.

We ate like kings that night, happy in completion of our hard work. We walked back to my cabin, drank some beers and fell asleep on the floor, promising to do it all again tomorrow.

Heroes

To some people running is a sort of a religion. Out here on the road they find their church, their penance and their peace.

In that respect, I suppose Pheidippides, the ancient Greek,

is a sort of patron saint. It was he who ran the first marathon, bringing the news of the Athenian victory over the Persians at the Battle of Marathon. It is the origin story of our sport, the foundation myth which every runner knows.

It's said that when he completed his task running those forty-odd kilometres, he shouted the word 'Joy' and then died. He is the first great hero of running but there are countless others. Abebe Bikila is one of them.

Bikila was a no-fuss man, a runner's runner, a Hemingway of the feet. He was the first great East African marathon athlete and won the 1960 Rome Olympics barefoot.

When I watch old videos of his races there is a grace in his movement, a lightness to his run. His body shape, his footfall, it all shouts runner.

That he won the 1960 Olympic marathon was something, but to come back the next Olympics, break his own record and become, in the process, the first back-to-back winner of marathon gold – well that was legend-making stuff.

Without him there is no Tergat, no Gebrselassie (and these are icons of the sport); without him the sport would be a poorer thing.

Bikila, like Pheidippides, was to live a short life: hurt in a terrible car accident in 1969 he never walked again. The injuries, though paralysing him from the waist down, did not extinguish his competitive spirit and he competed in other sports before dying four years later aged only forty-one.

He received a state funeral in his native Ethiopia with

Emperor Haile Selassie declaring a national day of mourning. Sixty-four thousand people lined the streets to bid the man farewell.

Before his death he spoke of it being God's will that he both win the Olympics and be hurt in that car accident. He said that he had to accept both the victory and tragedy as facts of life and live happily.

I relate to Bikila as much as I can with any runner. The son of a shepherd, he did not run until his mid-twenties. We both, it seems, share this small piece of biography together; running farmers, moving towards some larger goal, he the Olympic medal, I the dream of being a writer.

I have come too to respect, as he called it, the will of life, the will of God; accidents befall us, health fails, relationships end but there is always the hope in tomorrow. Perhaps, I think, after all I have encountered, I did not choose running: it chose me.

Warming up the engine

I've run about 5k now and I've hit my stride. My legs move without my thinking, I no longer need to control my pace or rhythm. My body knows what to do.

In the last few years of running, as my body has grown fitter and stronger, I've found a curious thing; namely it takes me a long time to get into a run. The first four or so kilometres can be a real pain, a real effort and push where I have to think about a whole host of things. Am I going too fast? Can I keep this pace? Did I eat enough? Drink enough? Can I do this? Is this going to be a good run?

That last question is probably the biggest and most unpredictable of all. In truth I don't think any runner knows the answer. Some days, well, some days it's just not in you.

I've often blocked out the time, made the necessary arrangements on the farm to go for a long run, only to return just half an hour later, exhausted and feeling pretty much a failure. It's not a nice feeling but after a while you get used to it and begin to accept that your body does indeed have limitations. It's not a sign of weakness, in fact in some cases it's a sign of over-training, overdoing things.

I used to train every single day, hitting the track and gym for maybe thirteen days straight. I was thin as a rake, reduced to just lean muscle, but life had become a little too regimented, a little too serious and strict.

Running had become a chore, a box to be ticked each day, it had become a sort of job that brought less pleasure with each outing.

I've seen it happen since with other friends, when their whole life became overtaken with the run, the addiction of the task. Replacing one bad habit with another and turning the simple act of running into an unhealthy thing.

They say the getting of wisdom comes through mistakes; if that's the case then I'm a very wise man indeed and I've learned now to enjoy the run for what it is. Some call it free running – there is no need for times, or watches, you run simply for joy.

My engine is warmed up now. I've barely broken a sweat. I'm in good form. I move on, happy and confident. The run is with me today and I'm glad.

Come and get your love

Running to music is just about as good as life can get. I'm a crooner at heart. I hit the low notes and make silly voices when I sing. When I run, well, you're likely to hear me before you see me.

I'm listening to Redbone's 'Come And Get Your Love' as I move out of the village. It's a great 70s hit from a Native American band. As I leave the graveyard and lake behind I shout the song's chorus, 'Come and get your love!' I'm playing air guitar now, as I run and sing, and it's such a joyous thing to be alive. I like to imagine all our dead neighbours are looking down and smiling, saying that at least one of us has got the right idea and is enjoying this thing called life.

Music can lift a run, and bring a runner back from the dead.

Different music helps at different times in a run. Often a slow techno beat can get one started off: it's repetitive and mechanical, it's like a train leaving from a station, picking up speed. Hip hop keeps you motivated and feeling like a tough guy when you face those major hills. But when I've hit my stride, such as now, I like to listen to something happy. 70s and 80s hits really do make you feel good when the sun's on your back and the wind's in your hair. It's a simple thing and a joyous thing.

I've shared some of life's great moments with Sting and the Police, Dire Straits and Earth, Wind and Fire. A corny bunch, but by God can you sing along to them.

A few months ago I spent two weeks living by the sea in Ibiza. I was there writing and every evening I ran out by the salt lakes of Salinas heading towards the sea. Each evening's run was accompanied by classic hits from an old-time Spanish rock station, Melodia FM.

I'd finish writing at five, put on my running gear and hit the motorway. It was a 10k run from the road to the beach, along which there happened to be a national park where migrating flamingos from Africa fed for the season.

The setting sun proved a welcome balm for my stiff joints as Sting and the Police played 'Roxanne' for the second evening in a row.

Ibiza is a beautiful island. On the roadside wild figs and vineyard grapes grow in plentiful supply and as I hit the 5k mark, I'd grab a bunch and crunch them in my mouth, savouring their juicy flesh as tourists whizzed by in open-top cars and scooters.

At the sea I'd run into the water, swim twenty laps and turn for home.

The radio station would never fail to impress and some great 80s guitar-driven hit would wind me home, singing loud and clear, the sea water drying in my hair as I ran in the cool evening sun. An Irishman, on a Spanish road, shouting to American songs.

The road

I've left the village behind. Passing the France road I look towards our neighbours' land. The Charters family lost much in the last generation; three sons to three different tragedies: the War of Independence, the *Titanic* and the Battle of the Somme.

William, Robert and David Charters were younger men than I am now when death took them. I cannot know what their dreams of this world were but I imagine we shared similar goals; to have a wife, a family, some land and make a living.

I have written elsewhere of William's death in the War of Independence, forming a short story to give him a decent end, one that was denied him in life, for he was assassinated by the IRA over a claimed informant role and dumped in a nearby lake.

David, who drowned on the *Titanic*, has a special connection to me, too, for my great-grand-aunt was on the same vessel. Katie Mullen survived with the help of a local man, James Farrell, getting on board the very last lifeboat, only to see her neighbours James and David die. She never crossed the waters of the Atlantic again, the memory too much for her.

Of Robert and the Somme I have yet to write something. But I will.

That the three brothers should have been taken before their time is a great sadness, but that they be forgotten would be a far worse thing indeed. To be Irish is to have the burden of history upon us and yet I think now it is no great burden to remember these three fine young men. In another world we could all of us have been friends, we are all of us native sons.

I pick up steam and hum the words of an old warrior song come to me. I am sure the Irish men of Robert's company knew the refrain of the famous 'Óró, sé do bheatha 'bhaile', a rebel marching song. It is an old air from the Jacobite wars of Bonnie Prince Charlie and at times I sing it as I move along.

The song sings to Gráinne Mhaol, a pirate queen who, having been hurt and sold to foreigners, returns with fighting Gaels by her side to rout the foreigners from our lands now that summer's come.

I imagine Robert chiming it as his company marched out of some training camp in Dublin or England ready to fight the Boche, full of optimism that the great push would this time work. That Haig and his companions would not direct them wrong this time. The lions led by donkeys.

This stretch of road, I must admit, always makes me think of war, for just round the bend there is a strange connection that life, but not novelists, can allow.

I do not know if Field Marshal Sir Henry Wilson knew young Robert Charters or if he read his name in the list of the dead from the Somme, but perhaps he saw the familiar address of Ballinalee and paused some morning in his war-time barrack.

Henry Wilson was born in Currygrane House just out-side the village and remains a pivotal character in the history of Empire. Born in 1864 to an Anglo-Irish family, Wilson's father had been a large landowner in the area, High Sher-iff and Deputy Lieutenant. Henry joined the army in 1882 aged just eighteen: it would be his home for the rest of his life.

Wilson's military career is that of the Empire at its peak. Posted to India in 1885 on a long-sought-for commission, he then served in the Third Burmese war.

That war was to mark the final conquering of all of Burma and its total annexation by the British. Soldiers and officials took loot and the conquering army sent back gold, jewellery and silks, which were presented to the royal family as gifts.

Wilson's time was spent in fighting a counter-insurgency war to quell Burmese resistance. Burma had proved to be a hugely costly exercise for the British, with the First Burmese War costing somewhere around £40 billion in today's money. It was obvious then that the Empire would not give up on its ambition. The Burmese monarchy was overthrown and their last king Thibaw forced on a bullock cart through the royal capital's street before living the rest of his life in exile.

Henry was wounded in Burma and convalesced in India and then Ireland. It must have been strange for him to return to Ballinalee after his tiger-hunting days but I imagine, too, that perhaps he had some shock from all that he had seen, and peaceful Longford, with its winding lanes and friendly faces, must have been a welcome sight.

He continued his military studies and graduated from staff college in 1893, being then promoted to captain. It was during this time that he became a protégé of Earl Roberts, then a major military figure who would become Commander in Chief of India and later Ireland and then led the British forces in the Second Boer War.

Wilson's career reads as a *Who's Who* entry of imperial might. Joining the intelligence service, he became the youngest staff officer in the British army at thirty-one.

Using his connections, he helped devise a plan of attack against the Boer before himself travelling to Africa to take part in the fighting and later joining Earl Roberts' staff.

The Boer fought bitterly and though they lost the conventional war their guerrilla war continued for many years.

It was here in South Africa that the first concentration camp was developed, with the victorious British rounding up the Boer. Forty-five of these camps were built with 115,000 people imprisoned: 28,000, mostly women and children, died in them as well as a further 20,000 native black Africans.

The move had been used to force the still fighting guerrillas to fully surrender. It would earn the British an infamy and plant the seeds for future would-be empires to round up the innocent.

We would perhaps never know the true figures of deaths if it had not been for Emily Hobhouse, an English campaigner who brought it to the world's attention. She herself would later be tarnished by the British government as a traitor for her work.

That Wilson knew of the concentration camps is a certainty but that he played an active role in developing the idea of them we do not know. History has certain secrets. Still, perhaps one day I shall know.

By 1910 Wilson had become Director of Military Operations at the British War Office and was preparing for a war on the Continent. A supporter of conscription and Ulster Unionism, he was to play a pivotal role in the history of modern Ireland.

He supported the Northern Unionists in their opposition to the Third Home Rule Bill, which was due to be passed in 1914, giving Ireland a parliament and form of self-control of its own. Under Wilson's friendship, the gun returned to Irish politics when the Northern Unionists imported rifles and formed armies and squadrons to fight with force, if necessary, the Home Rule Bill, which the British government would enforce if enacted. They were British, they said, and did not seek to leave the Union.

Wilson felt so strongly about the whole affair and his refusal to send British troops against British men that he helped instrument the Curragh incident, when dozens of British army officers tendered their resignation rather than fight against Ulster loyalists. The British responded by backing down and insisting the whole affair had been a misunderstanding.

The Curragh incident was to prove a turning point in the self-determination of Irish nationalism as nationalists realised they would never receive fair treatment from Britain and that

Home Rule itself, though passed, would most likely never happen.

Their fears were right as the Bill was suspended at the outbreak of the Great War. Tens of thousands of Irish men would go on to fight in the war, some dying for a free Ireland, others for a united kingdom.

Wilson would continue his own rise in the now-at-war army, leading men and troops, and at the end of the four years of bloodshed he became Britain's chief military adviser at the Paris Peace Conference of 1919. For his work he was promoted to Field Marshal by Churchill.

There is no statue, no monument nor plaque to this most famous man in Ballinalee. Even Currygrane House, his home place, no longer stands for it was burned by the IRA. I do not know how I feel about this man. His allegiances are not my own, his actions, his choices, alien to me. His rise to power is, however, an impressive thing but one that makes me feel unease, for it was built on bloodshed. His was a name I did not know for many years but one I cannot now ever forget.

My father has told me that, when back in Longford, Wilson and his family would ride their buggy through the village and the people would bow and take off their hats to them. That image has stayed with me more than all the accolades and pomp.

I wonder now, with all his power and influence, if he could not have pulled young Robert Charters from the doomed Somme? They were both Anglo-Irish, both Protestants, both neighbours. I wonder, with all his might, if he could not have found some safer harbour for the young man? In the long black train of history and reflection perhaps there was a time when he too thought that.

Wilson's story does not finish here but I've had enough of war for now and put my mind once more to the road. I don't feel much like singing war songs any more. History, at a distance of a thousand years, is safe, for we are not much affected by the deaths of men in the long ago, but history of the recent world is not the same; it is all too close, all too real.

A break in the clouds

The sun has moved behind the clouds and the day has grown somewhat paler. To run in Ireland is to inhabit the weather. Rain and weather have a big effect on my farming life and so too it's true with my running one.

The weather this spring is pleasant but the just passed winter has been a long one. It was not so wet as last year but the darkness caught me unprepared again. Our light carries only from 8am to about 4 in the winter. It is a tough time to be a runner, for with work and farming there are precious little hours of daylight left to get out on the road.

Running and working out in the rain in Ireland is pretty much an inevitable thing. You are going to get rained on, that's just a fact, and once you get over that you can get on with life. I don't much mind running in the rain any more, but there comes a time in the middle of the winter when things are just too wet and grey and cold and you need to move indoors.

In those times I migrate to the gym. It's bright, warm and full of like-minded people. I call my gym runs the twenties. Every day, I do a short twenty-minute run on the treadmill, then I hit the weights.

To be a good runner you need to use weights too, to make your body stronger. I carry out my core exercises, my pull-ups and push-ups, then I hit the bars and free weights. Since becoming a runner my body has changed. It has become a muscular thing, a sought-for thing. We must inhabit our bodies, as Emerson said, and in so doing we can build a new life.

It is my engine and I treat it properly now, putting only healthy food in it. There were times I did not love this, my only vehicle, but not any more. Now I give thanks in the celebration of the self.

It's something my girlfriend Vivian jokes about, saying, 'Who said you can't be intellectual and ripped?' I imagine myself some modern-day Whitman or Thoreau, a farmer writer from the middle of Ireland ready to take on the critics and woo the audiences. Well that's the plan, anyway.

It's a fun daydream and it's good to dream for it keeps me company on these long runs.

I'm warmed up but not too warm to take off my jumper. If it rains I'll be ready. Hopefully the sun will return. It's been such a good day so far.

I'm leaving the orbit of my small universe now as I move

out the winding road. Past the piggery and the Shepherd Brady's fields I move. I've many bends and turns in front of me before I hit Edgeworthstown some 12k away.

Little league

I still remember my first 5k race. I was nervous and worried. Worried that I might not be able to finish the event, that I'd be embarrassed in front of the other competitors.

Every race has its caste system. The professionals are up the front. You can tell them by their nice outfits and lean lithe bodies. Then the fitness fanatics, who have the endurance but not the talent of professionals, then comes your dad bod character who's fit but getting on a bit and runs just a couple evenings a week. The dad bods are then followed by the rest of us: a mishmash of middle-aged mums, keep-active seniors and children. It's a fine social order and by and large we all respect our place in the queue.

There are, however, the madmen. The madmen are wild cats who place themselves right at the starting line, ready and waiting to go. They've got the energy to match the professionals for a bit and drive the rest of us to near lunacy.

They're not pace-setters – that would make too much sense – no, they're just lunatics who tear off at a blistering pace for about a kilometre and then promptly drop out, tired, wheezing and wondering why they couldn't keep it up.

You meet them in every race, you might even get caught

by them once or twice, but you'll never do it again because to play their games means you, too, will run out of gas.

Gas is important when you're competing. It's the fuel you've got inside you that allows you to know roughly how long you can run for. Gas is a sort of a one-fill operation; when it's gone it's gone. Like undertaking a long car ride, you have to pace yourself. You can't just punch it the whole way there.

The madmen taught me a lot about gas that first race.

It was a few years ago now and I'd graduated from the treadmill to outdoor running. I was still very much a newbie, coming to grips with my body, with what it could do. I didn't know my limits and I knew nothing about gas.

The race, a simple 5k, had a nice gathering of a hundred or so people. I lined up near the start wanting to get a good place and not wanting to get caught behind some slow children. I was nervous and not very focused and when the gun went off I darted out with the madmen. We ran with heart and might for a kilometre, each trying to outdo the other. There was a point for maybe a minute or so where I even thought I might win this race and then my gas tank started to flash and beep. Lactic acid built up in my shoulders and my breathing grew heavy. I looked around me and my fellow competitors were also showing the same signs; we began to wheeze and splutter like old cars and suddenly our pace began to drop and the fitness freaks showed up moving like racehorses through our flanks, depleting us with each pass, thundering across the track like some ancient steed.

Many of the madmen dropped out. I had been sabotaged and I was annoyed. I slowed but I didn't stop. I wasn't going to throw away my first 5k for the sake of hitting it too soon.

I slipped back and back into the race pack, finally settling in with the general public. It was here that I found I could keep pace.

The race organisers had water tables arranged and I grabbed a cup and calmed down. I gave myself a short pep talk there and then on the road and agreed we'd finish whatever it took.

It was also about this time I realised that all my fellow competitors were now retirees and that I was amongst the silver foxes. It was here that a sixty-year-old beat me to the finish line.

There's a special kind of kick in the guts when an old man beats you in a race, but he beat me fair and square.

He was a decent man and stopped to talk to me after it was all over.

'Was this your first race?' he enquired.

I nodded silently.

'Well, I've been running for forty years, so don't feel bad, you did good lad, the secret is to keep at it, pace yourself and sign up for the next race straight away. Don't give up.'

We shared a cup of tea and a banana then, and he told me how he had recently recovered from cancer and that running was the thing he had missed in his recovery time. He seemed to me the real victor of the race that day, a humble ordinary man who had overcome his own troubles to be there. He ran with a purpose and pride all of his own. He taught me something important that day. There are many stories out there on the road, feats of quiet greatness, accomplishments of pride and joy, and that we all must run with something in our hearts – it's what I think keeps us moving.

I haven't forgot that old-timer and I've learned a lot since that first 5k. The madmen never caught me off guard again and I've barely missed a day of running since.

It's not that it gets easier, no, it's that you find a strength you never knew you had.

Today is the big event

Dr George Sheehan was a great runner. I'm thinking of him now on this run. As much as the ancient Greeks started this whole marathon business, George added to it, making this world infinitely richer.

A track star in his college days, he abandoned the sport for a life in the medical profession. He only started running again at forty-five, proving once and for all that there's hope for even the latest comers to this sport.

Sheehan was a gifted writer and it's down to his writing and personable manner that thousands of Americans took up the running bug in the 1970s. He toured and talked around the world about his deep love of the road.

I discovered him a year ago and he's influenced how I see

things. As much as Thoreau showed me that Birchview, our farm, was my Walden, Sheehan has taught me that any road is the road to life. That today's the big event.

Running, as a philosophy, teaches us to live in the present moment, to be in the now. To me, God is in the natural world in the everyday, he is the first suckle of a newborn calf and the dying breath of an old mare. He is there in the quiet footfall over a morning road and the beauty of a sunset sprint.

Sheehan remarked that the body was treated like a second-class citizen in today's world. And yet are we not our bodies? Are we not this present moment? We must, we need, to recapture this great vehicle and reunite it with our minds. As he said himself, no life can be lived completely without being lived on a physical level.

The digital self I see now cannot give, with each post we become something less, something poorer. We seek attention from the other to make us feel more whole but in doing so we only deplete ourselves. If the great data towers of the now were ripped down, perhaps then we might see, truly see, the wonders before us, the wonders of the everyday, and live life not through our screens but through our senses.

Sheehan talked of finding your play through sport, any sport, and being a good animal. Exercise, he wrote, is one way to be that animal. In that line of thinking I like to imagine myself a lion; I stalk these roads ready to pounce, and in that image I've found my play, as silly as that might sound. I've got something that makes me happy, that brings me joy. I run and tire myself to find a peace in my body to quell that relentless restlessness. It might sound odd but it works for me.

George Sheehan died in 1993 of prostate cancer, running until his legs could no longer carry him.

He's with me today, whispering some words in my ear, like a Plato of the feet.

Today is our masterpiece, today is my Caravaggio.

Blowin' in the Wind

I pass the road for Corbeagh lake and think now that the day is fine for fishing, the sun is not too hot, the wind not too strong and there seems a healthy supply of insects in the air. The fish will bite today.

Us midlands people are a landlocked nation but we have been blessed with lakes in abundance. They are our links to water and being from a limestone region, I think now that they are visible representation of our porous landscape and porous souls.

I like Corbeagh lake, it is small but deep, there is a small boat house on it and I've fished it many times. There are perch and pike in its black waters but I've yet to catch any.

It was a few years ago now that I brought my friend Billy Maynard to fish this water. He had flown over from Germany to spend some time on the farm. It was a cold winter's day when we set out and we brought whiskey and sandwiches to keep us warm. We talked on the lake then of life and what he would do now that he was in Ireland. There was much he wanted to see, including a visit to the border with the North and to pour a pint of Guinness in a real Irish pub. We shall do it all, I promised, and we did.

We got no bites that day, the fish, I think, favouring to stay in the deep, but on my second or third casting, as I held the line taut on my finger, the wind blew and I could hear the line sing in the breeze; it was a new sound to me and a beautiful one, like some siren's call.

The song of the line has stayed with me now and I replay it in my mind. The thing about fishing is it's not about the fish, it's everything else. Perhaps when my run is done I will call Da and we shall take to the waters of Gowna or the Camlin, perhaps this evening we shall be lucky.

Moat Farrell

By bends and small hills I move now past the old post office. I pass a strong oak that took the life of a neighbour in a car crash and move on towards the Moat of Farrell.

Ireland is an ancient land littered with the remains of a thousand different lives, from the Stone Age peoples who built our portal tombs to the castles of the Gaels and later Normans. In Moat Farrell there lies an old mound, the seat of a chieftain.

Towering high above the road, it is the highest point for ten miles and affords a view of this part of Longford.

Once, in the long ago, Longford was known by another

name: Annaly. It was ruled by the chieftains of the Farrell clan. This was their Camelot. It's said that new chieftains were brought to this mound to be inaugurated. A Revd Joseph McGivney wrote that it was here that the new lord took his seat. Surrounded by bishops, abbots, sub-chiefs and poets, the ancient rites were performed. The chieftain was given a wand upon the inaugural throne, the wand being straight, to symbolise his carrying out his office with straight dealings, and white, that he should be pure and without stain.

The new chieftain would then turn three times to the right and three times to the left to mark the holy Trinity and a sandal was placed on his foot by the chief marshal, showing his submission to the new lord, the Christian God.

The Farrells are mentioned in the ancient *Annals of the Four Masters*, a record of medieval Ireland, but it was under King James I that they finally lost their control over Longford to the English.

Landless, the clan members became part of what was known as the Flight of the Wild Geese, the movement of Irish Catholic gentry and soldiers to fight in the armies of Continental Europe. They returned briefly to fight in the Irish Confederate War of 1641. That war was a last-ditch attempt by the native Catholic gentry to wrest control from the colonising English. The rebellion was a failure and ultimately led to the Cromwellian genocide which saw the first real modern acts of ethnic cleansing in Western Europe. Out of a pre-war population of 1.5 million, 41 per cent of the population were killed by violence, ethnic cleansing and famine. Thousands of the surviving people were then rounded up and forcibly sent to the Caribbean to work the growing plantations in a practice known as Barbadosing. It's interesting to note that in Jamaica there is a Longford Road, a visible reminder of those deported thousands. They are our long-lost cousins across the waters.

Many have argued that the Cromwellian actions were an effort to finally eliminate the Irish, thereby freeing up the land for English settlers. What began with Cromwell was in many ways repeated in other British colonies, from the Americas to Australia; namely the clearing of a land and the creation of a *Terra nullius*, a landscape that could be remade.

It was here, too, that the sub-humanisation of the Irish began. By reducing the humanity of the Gael to a lower form, actions which were otherwise unthinkable could now be allowed to take place. The savage did not count.

It was Ireland that proved the test tube for the actions of Empire that would occur around the globe.

The Moat, or Motte, is all that remains now, wild and overrun with grass, the last remnants of an ancient clan. The descendants of the Farrells are scattered across the globe from Spain to Mexico.

Running farmers

The farmland around Moat Farrell is fine rolling pasture. Cattle happily eat from their green beds and watch me pass.

There's nothing quite like the smell of spring meadows; the wild garlic flowers are growing and pockets of buttercups adorn the verge and fields.

Some of the best farmers I know are great runners. Moving cattle requires fitness. Cattle don't like dogs and will stand their ground and fight, so in rural Ireland we move them by hand through fields and along roads. More than once as a child I thought myself a hound for I've often chased after escaping bulls and marauding cows.

A cow can run flat out anywhere from twenty to thirty miles an hour. They can be slow to get moving so your only hope is to set off before they do. We can't outrun them but we can outsmart them and in the end that's all we've got going for us.

In my youth our farmland was not connected to our house, which meant as children we had to move them by hand to their summer pastures. This required a full mobilisation of my siblings, parents, bicycles, neighbours and a good deal of running. It was a bovine fiesta.

We would gather our troops on the chosen day, the children on bikes as my father and mother instructed us where to go. The cows, waiting to be let out to their new summer grass, would low excitedly from the farmyard knowing what was to come. My mother would then walk down to the main road and man the bad bend to the left of our house, slowing traffic and people. My brother or our neighbour and friend Gary would position himself atop his family's lane next door and the battle would begin.

There's a strange sense of power when you have control of a public road, even if it is only for a short time. Vacant of cars it becomes something else, something different, a highway to some other place.

There was a link to a quite ancient thing in our practice then that we did not know, for the very roads themselves, *bóthar*, 'the cow way', are based on the ancient pathways of cattle.

More than once I jogged behind the stock on these treks. The journey of some three kilometres was slow and the cattle often tried to break away or turn back for home. It was as epic as the crossing of the American west to us then. After probably a half hour we'd reach the fabled land of Kilnacarrow where the summer ground lay.

My young body tired and sweaty, I'd relax on a gate and admire the beasts, our beasts, as they grazed on their sweet summer grass. They were, I think now, the first real runs I ever did.

Charlton's Folly

I am on the Edgeworthstown road good and proper now. I know this road well for as a teenager I travelled it often with my father in his work van. I can still walk its bends and nooks in my mind, in a patrol of the imagination.

My father is a great lover of history and it's through him and those van rides that I've learned so much of the story of my home. Past the Moat of Farrell and the grazing cattle I move by an old graveyard. I cannot fully see it from here but I have entered the land of Charlton's Folly.

It's but an overgrown ruin now and yet it remains a plaque to the memory of lost love. In the long ago, Thomas Charlton, a member of the local Anglo-Irish gentry and landowner in Longford and Meath, was set to die an old bachelor, leaving all his fortune to his extended family. However, at the age of seventy-five, he met and fell in love with a local young woman.

Charlton's joy was such that he immediately began to build their new home, but before the wedding could be consummated and Charlton produce an heir, his young bride died. (Others say the marriage was prevented from happening.) Heartbroken, Charlton changed his will on his deathbed in 1792, bequeathing his entire fortune to a fund for love, Charlton's Charity. Its purpose was simple: to give a small payment to young couples who were to marry in order that they might have a helping start in life.

The unfinished house stands upon the landscape still, reminding me of my own lost loves, of roads not taken and lives not lived. Charlton's love outlived him and in the process became legend, and perhaps that is the greatest gift anyone could ask for: that love might blossom anew again and again from tragedy.

And bend and stretch

Past the ruins I run now. I'm nearing my physiotherapist's house. Collette is a no-nonsense woman. She's treated all the men of our family and reminds me that we are all prone to a bad back. Visiting her is part therapy and part playful abuse, for she scolds and slags me for every injury I accrue.

The fact I am running on the road today won't make her happy, for she has warned me time and again 'to stay off the fecking tarmac'.

Clocking up seventy to a hundred kilometres of running a week takes its toll on one's legs and I've hurt my knees, feet and ankles in the process. Through dry needling, sports massage and some helpful instruction Collette has brought me back from the dead countless times. She is a Lazarus of the legs.

I've been sticking to trail-running lately and I know this will make Collette happy for it's easier on my joints. If I hurt myself on the road today, she won't have sympathy for me because I've been warned of the hardship of the road, but she will fix me up as she has always done.

Through her I've come to appreciate good footwear. There was a time when any old runners would do for I didn't run very far, but it really pays to invest in a good pair of running shoes. Like car tyres, they need to be changed after a few hundred miles because they wear out easily and, like car tyres, it's probably best to have a spare set. I've found my latest runners to be an able match for the mileage I'm making and together we've tackled roads around the world.

Aside from a decent pair of shoes there are no other real costs to running. It is a recession-proof sport, one that needs no equipment, no fancy gear, no membership fees and can be done anywhere.

We are the running ape, in fact there is no other animal better at long distance than us. There's a certain species pride in that that brings a smile to my face.

Edgeworthstown

I'm on the long straight to Edgeworthstown now. There's not much traffic on my approach and I decide to refuel with one of my gels. I got caught recently on a half-marathon when I hadn't drunk enough liquids before I started. I was overseas and it was a hot day and through sweat and unpreparedness I had to stop at the 17k mark, buy some water and then get moving again. I'm a bit like a train when I run, I don't like stopping, seeing it as some sort of sign of weakness. Silly, I know, but that's how I am. The stoppage taught me a valuable lesson: that even now, after hundreds of races, each run is unique, each outing is different, with new challenges and problems to be surmounted.

I run at least one half-marathon every month; it keeps my fitness levels in check and I find it a great way to relax. The 20s, as I call the shorter runs, are great and you can get a nice

5k in, but in order to get some real thinking and down time you can't beat a long run.

I suck on my gel packet; it's almost sickly sweet with a sugary orange flavour. It refuels me and gives me the necessary sugars I need to keep my energy levels up. Food is life. We have a great value on it in this land.

I've been coming to Edgeworthstown most of my life. It's a one-street town typical of the Irish midlands but it has a history all of its own.

I turn left at the Park House Hotel and make my way up Main Street. This place was once called Mostrim, but the ruling Anglo family titled it after themselves as was so often done in the past. The Edgeworth line is all but gone now but theirs is a story of invention, deposed kings and literature. I move up the town and can see the remains of their once-grand manor house. It's a nursing home now and it is here that my maternal grandmother passed away recently. I am forever now connected to the Edgeworths and to this place through Nana Reilly.

The historic house was built in 1672 by the Edgeworth family and greatly enlarged by Richard Lovell Edgeworth in the 1770s. Richard was a politician, inventor and writer and had pivotal connections with the ruling elites and intellectuals of not just Britain but the world itself. Through his long life and four marriages he fathered a staggering twenty-two children. A member of the intellectual group the Lunar Society, his inventions would be shared with members such as the discoverer of oxygen, Joseph Priestley, the founding father of America,

Benjamin Franklin, and Erasmus Darwin, slavery abolitionist and grandfather to Charles Darwin.

Through the members of the society, it's said that some of the central ideas of the industrial revolution began and indeed, through its informal meetings, some of the great inventions of the age were shared.

The enlightenment company had a positive effect on Edgeworth and he was an advocate of Catholic Emancipation, the social reform revolution led by Daniel O'Connell to grant voting rights to the native Irish and to remove the extremely harsh Penal Laws. Edgeworth was a man free of prejudice.

The tradition of intellectualism was to continue to many of Richard's children, including his daughter Lucy Jane, who would marry the astronomer Thomas Romney Robinson, who would give his name to the Robinson crater on the very moon itself.

His relation Abbé Edgeworth, also born in Edgeworthstown, would become the celebrated black sheep of the family, a convert to Catholicism and later a priest. He would hear the last confession of King Louis XVI before his execution.

Maria Edgeworth is now, however, the best remembered of the family. A long-lived novelist, she helped in the very formation of modern literature. Born in England, Maria came to live with her father in Edgeworthstown in 1773. A strong-willed and learned woman, she wrote not just fiction but on the role of women in managing estates and financial affairs.

Her friendships read as a *Who's Who* of eighteenth-century Europe: her neighbour and close friend Kitty Pakenham would become the wife of the Duke of Wellington. Her close comrade Sir Walter Scott, the creator of *Ivanhoe,* would be a long-time correspondent and dear friend, Lord Byron himself would hail her as a literary great, and economist David Ricardo, who made his fortune on betting on the outcome of the Battle of Waterloo, counted her as a confidante.

Maria's novels are not so much remembered today but in her time she was hailed as even greater than Jane Austen. *Castle Rackrent* and *The Absentee* both tell the stories of absentee landlords and rack-renting ruling elites (the charging of exorbitant rents). *Rackrent* was rightly seen as the first historical novel and also one of the first regional novels which had vernacular speech of the local Irish contained within, so it was that the Longford lexicon entered the world of literature.

The Absentee is a deeply political work and portrayed the real living conditions of the native Irish and the lives of their British masters. A hugely brave work for its time, it pulled at the very heart of aristocratic and ruling England.

And yet for all of her political awareness Maria herself is a conflicted character, a one-time anti-Semite (she later apologised for her remarks) and at times has a superior view of the native Irish.

An Gorta Mór

There is, in my home, a missing portion of people. The land, the place, is quiet: it is quiet because nearly 75,000 people are not there.

When the Famine struck Longford, we had a population of some 115,000. Today, it is just above 40,000. Thomas Francis Meagher, the Irish revolutionary and leader of the Fighting 69th in the American Civil War, referred to it as the skeleton at the table. The skeleton of the ghost people.

As a child I remember working in the fields with my father. We were digging holes for new fencing on the farm and I found the remains of an old shoe. 'You have to be careful where you dig here,' he told me; 'the dead are all around us.'

Maria Edgeworth's actions of that time are at once noble and infuriating. She wrote her novel *Orlandino* to raise funds worldwide for my starving forebears and her writings provide some of the accounts of the famine in Longford. It's thanks to her servant Biddy Macken that we have oral testimony to her giving of charity and indeed her actions led to foodstuffs being sent from America to provide relief.

However, the conflict of Edgeworth and her peers becomes apparent when it's noted that some landlords only gave alms to those of their tenants who had paid their rent, an almost impossible task in a famine lasting several years.

She said, too, that she had a preference that people work for their alms: 'to excite the people to work for good wages, and not, by feeding gratis, to make beggars of them, and ungrateful beggars, as the case may be.' Her views are at odds with how we view humanitarian disasters now.

She watched as hundreds poured through the town emaciated, broken, walking in search of something else. They walked away from one life and ended in another as a dislocated people. Edgeworth would die before the famine ended and, despite all her fundraising, thousands more would pass away. Lamenting to her last about the poor, she said: 'Ireland, with all thy faults, thy follies too, I love thee still'.

That the Famine was in and of itself a willed genocide has been debated for two centuries. The fact that other foods were grown and exported in the black years and not given to the most in need tell us of the attitude of the Empire towards its subjects. That landlords, the administrators of that Empire, evicted whole villages of people and shipped them around the world in order to open up grazing land for livestock tells us all we need to know of the motivations of the elite of that day.

Tony Blair himself issued an apology for the moral crimes of the Empire in the Famine, saying it was the defining event in the history of Ireland and of Britain and that it still causes pain as we reflect on it today.

'Those who governed in London at the time failed their people through standing by while a crop failure turned into a massive human tragedy.'

The Famine is the Zero Hour of Ireland's long history.

It is where all roads end and begin. It is where the clock of nationhood stops and starts. My grandfather's father was born just years after it. I wonder what stories they told around their tenant fireplace, what horrors had been seen. We Irish are all of us survivors of that time, the remnants of the million dead. We are the half shadow to the ghost people.

Britain harks back to the glory of Empire in its history programmes, to the honour of the Tudors, the spirit of Cromwell, the bulwark of Churchill and the never-setting sun, but to us, to the children of Empire, they are times of tragedy, the time of the historical amnesia where our sufferings are forgotten by the masters themselves.

For me to go back in history in some time machine is not a happy thought for me and the other peoples of Empire; things become only worse.

When I run through Longford I run over the remains of 75,000 ghosts. It is no wonder that one never truly feels alone here.

Inspiration

Every runner needs inspiration. I got mine a few weeks ago when my dear friend Father Sean brought me to an international athletics event in the next town.

At times I like to fancy myself a real runner and even in my daydreams think that my childhood promise, if it had been directed, might have resulted in me becoming a real athlete.

I was a fast kid, there's no denying that, but what I saw a few weeks ago ended that lingering daydream for ever.

Real athletes are a cut apart, they move differently, run differently and seem to inhabit a different world.

Father Sean and I didn't really know what to expect when we arrived at the Athlone International Grand Prix but we had been told that tonight there would be an attempt at some world records and that we were in for an evening of entertainment.

The indoor track at Athlone Institute of Technology is state of the art, a beautiful free-flowing thing with vaulted ceilings and just plain comfy stadium seats. We settled in with some water and snacks and watched as the first of the events began.

Runners from America, Canada, Jamaica and Kenya lined up and before I knew it I had been transported to another dimension.

Seeing their beautiful chiselled bodies perform feats of hurdles, sprints, long jumps and high jumps awed and astounded me.

We read their race records in our booklet and made fun wagers as to who would do the biz, with Father Sean winning on some and I on others.

It was in the running of the indoor mile towards the end of the night that things got really heated. The track record was going to be broken tonight and there was a hope that a world record might be thrown down.

The men gathered at the starting line right in front of us. They were, we remarked, about my age and yet had already lived lifetimes. In their lean forms was the history of a thousand training days, of the sweat of victory and the smell of defeat. I gazed in wonder as they set off and at the pace at which they moved.

I'm a slow starter in a race as I want to conserve that gas, but these men, they ran as if they were made of gas, there was no easing in, it was adrenaline from the off. Rounding each corner we cheered as our favoured runner inched up the line, passing men on either side as they circled. We heard the thunder of their feet upon the turf, clopping like runaway horses, each footfall timed and perfect.

Form in running is something I had never really thought of until that night, but their movements were all of them calculated and the race was of the mind as much as that of the flesh. Each corner, each leg raise, each adjustment was a carefully thought-out thing. They were each of them scientists of movement.

As they rounded for the final stretch the leaders were clear and then the final surge came, men ran with everything, but it was not in some crazed abandon but rather the form of a professional, the form of an athlete.

We stood and cheered as everyone did that evening as the closing seconds of the closing race came. The winner was declared and we shared in the joy of it all as if it were we ourselves who had completed the feat.

I was changed as a runner that night, I was humbled and inspired. I know I'll never be a professional and probably never could have been but I still run and at times like to pretend some of those guys are racing with me. It's silly, I know, but every runner's gotta dream.

Father Sean and I have talked of it since with great joy. We have never seen anything quite like it.

The man who made time isn't making any more of it

Running takes time. I'm not talking about the amount of hours you are out there on the road but rather the making of that time in your busy life, the clearing of a schedule, the 5am alarm-clock siren, the cold winter evenings on your own. Running is a mistress that cannot be ignored and time is her chariot.

Running requires a self-willed discipline, namely that we have to put it above our other needs for a few minutes every day. You really want to go home and watch Netflix after work? Well how about first you get your arse out on the road for a half-hour and then you can go and watch *Rick and Morty* or *Chef's Table* or whatever it is you're into. It can be a pain to make this time but ultimately, no matter how tired or cranky you are when you take those first steps, you finish feeling better. In the expounding of energy we gain new life.

For the last while I haven't had the luxury of real running. I was working a job that paid the bills but that took all of my time from me. My running life was reduced and resized into small snitches, curtailed visits to treadmills and maybe a long run at the weekend. This was, I knew, a test of my active life.

One could simply abandon it, saying I am too busy, or one could find ways around it.

The idea of runs kept me going. Like the flashes of inspiration for stories in my writing life, images of me out there on a track came to me and bred in me new hunger. I would endure five days of repetitive evening treadmills in the gym to capture one great day of a long run in the woods or along a riverbank or up a mountain.

I would make the time count when it did come. As Seneca said, we must seize what flees.

I recently heard the singer Noel Gallagher talk about creative ideas coming down from the heavens and that if we are not ready to receive them they will move on to someone else. I think that is true for runs too. The *aisling* or dream vision of a great run will move on to another runner if we are not willing to take them.

It might sound odd, but then why do people go on running holidays or enter adventure races? Each step is in and of itself an act of creation, each finished race a dream imagined and fulfilled. We are our own wish-fulfilling jewels. For even the most normal of runners it is the image of us crossing the finishing line that keeps us going. We are all of us artists of the feet.

My busy job taught me to appreciate time and maybe in a way how to hold on to dreams too.

All creatures great and small

I've left Edgeworthstown behind me and am moving out on a long straight road to Granard. I run past the local national school and see the children still inside their classroom and smile.

Sunlight flows gently upon me as above birds dart and play, catching small insects. One sees all of nature on a run in the countryside, from wildflower-strewn ditches to hunting otters on riverside banks.

The road can be a place of death and life, from where murders of crows pick over the remains of rabbits, to brave hedgehogs slowly surmounting its black expanse in search of new homes. The road, this place, is both beautiful and sad, a space of endings and beginnings.

As a farmer I have always loved nature. Connected and bound as we are to the seasons and environment, we are custodians of it too and must protect it for not just ourselves but the greater mass of society.

We runners get to observe life in the slow lane; unencumbered of cars and mechanical transport we can just stop should a thing take our fancy or indeed if the glory of the world comes upon us. It was on a run like today's that I came across my own private Constable.

The murmuration of starlings is one of the wonders of rural Ireland. The flocking group of hundreds of small birds across the sky is like an aerial shoal. As gentle and fierce as spilling water, they form and break and roll along the air like the floating notes of an unheard symphony. They are as a million Gershwin crescendos fluttering and crashing upon us.

Their movements were recently described by experts and journalists in a well-known US science magazine in the form of equations of 'critical transitions', namely systems that are poised to become something else, that these birds are more akin to the instant transformation of, say, liquids turning to gas or metals becoming magnetised. They are creatures caught in a moment of creation.

Like the electrons of a chemical element each bird in the murmuration is connected to its neighbour, leading to the entire turn of a flock in unison in what's known as a phase transition.

Each bird moves together in one huge large-scale pattern change across the sky, but experts do not know how a bird on the opposite end of a flock that could consist of thousands of members can simultaneously know to turn. Some experts have argued that the movement is a point of biological critic-ality that works on the interaction of neurons and cells. That they operate, in other words, on a level of universal principles in acts greater than we can understand.

If landscape can hold history and neurons can fire mem-ories then perhaps these murmurations are what the synapse of memory looks like, folding back onto itself for ever and ever in an infinite loop, holding love, loss and happiness.

I remember the evening as I ran below this swarming mass

of life and I thought not of science, nor the electrons, but the link of man to the divine, to the spiritual world, the greater world around us, and in that moment the cacophony of history ceased and all was one, united. Caught in beauty. One could look at them and see oneself reflected.

You can see a lot when you are out for a run. Sometimes, if you're lucky, you might even see the soul of the world.

The sympathetic nod

Mac DeMarco plays in my ears as I battle this straight. The road is quiet and the view is a long one. I can see the distance ahead of me and I try to think of other things. Long straights can be hard, I don't know why.

I begin to play air guitar to Mac's song 'Freaking Out the Neighborhood' as I shout out the lyrics.

'Really, I'm fine, never been better got no job on the line.'

Mac's been a constant companion for the last few months since my friend Tarhan introduced me to his music. It's been my soundtrack as I've tried to make it as a writer, battle a job and keep farming. Mac's been a real swell guy, as he might say himself.

Out of nowhere a cyclist passes me and says hello.

'Grand day for it,' I say.

' 'Tis surely,' he replies, cycling on.

There's a few rules on the road here in Ireland and if you learn them you'll have a good time.

1. *We say hello to each other.*

   Runners as a tribe are pretty good at this. If you're out in the middle of a trail run in the middle of nowhere, hauling ass, and you come across another runner, then you better say hi. It'd be rude not to.

2. *The nod.*

   If you can't say hello for some reason the nod will do. It's a basic acknowledgement of your fellow runner and lets them know you know what it's all about.

3. *Warnings.*

   If you came across something bad you'll warn your fellow runners. There's a bad crash on the road about a mile back, there's a wild bear (highly unlikely in rural Ireland, but still) and on it goes.

4. *Cyclists are people too.*

   Cyclists share the road with us and by and large they are a good group of people. Give them a quick greeting – you might need them one day to get help.

5. *We don't like speeding cars.*

   Country roads are narrow and bending. We don't like speeding cars coming around corners because they might hit us.

6. *Wear reflectors.*

In autumn and winter light is a problem. You might think you'll be seen but chances are a driver won't see you until it's too late. If you're going out at dusk put on a high-vis vest. It might look silly but it could just save your life.

Mac's jizz-jazz melodies keep me flowing and moving as I move ever onwards. To a stranger it might seem odd and out of place but happiness, I have learned, is an estate of the mind and it's best we fill the acreage of the self with things that bring us joy.

I might not be able to sing but the road won't mind.

Night-time runs

There is something special about night-time running. The world becomes a different place, both smaller and larger.

Out there under the stars a runner can feel part of the cosmos if only for the briefest of moments.

Running at night is a new experience. Torch light or head lamp at the ready, the runner can take in a new vista.

I remember my first night-time runs in the countryside as a teenager up and down our lane. Above, the bats swooped and swanned in the darkness and I could feel their wings moving over me, searching for food, for a mate, for something perhaps

I did not know about. At times such as these I thought I heard their songs too.

In those early training days sound took on new meaning in the night; in the distance our neighbours' donkey called, the cattle in the shed chatted to one another and the wind played through the trees.

To run at night is to see and hear the world anew, to live in a sonic world if just for a moment, hearing your breath beat out the rhythm of this place, feeling for a new land.

To run at night is a journey into the unknown each time and perhaps that's why we like it so much.

Heroes

I'm not quite at the half-marathon point yet and despite the long unchanging road I'm doing fine. My pace is good and steady, my feet and legs aren't sore and I know I've got a whole lot of run in me.

When I'm in this state all types of thoughts come to me, ideas for novels, scenes from movies, philosophical ruminations, images of my family and sometimes darker things; bad times, failed lives, bitter loves. It's at moments like this that I speak out loud to my body.

I thank it for bringing me this far, for becoming so strong. Mine is a house of mirrors, for my outward strength, to me, is a reflection of my inner one. That long-sought-for and hard-won thing that can surmount mountains and form the bridges of love. It was not easily built, but then what is.

In becoming this rebuilt man, this athlete of the soul, I found inspiration from real people. Paula Radcliffe was one of them. The women's marathon world record-holder for sixteen years, she proved to me what can be done with hard work and self-willed belief.

What I like about Paula is that she wasn't a winner straight away, she had to put in the hard graft competing in cross-country and shorter distances. She surmounted injuries, asthma and anaemia and in many a way was a journeyman wanderer before finding her true calling.

I have had points like that in my life, the so-close moments, the knockbacks, the rejection and the near career-ending failures. You have to run a lot of bad races before you start to win, likewise you write a lot of bad words in order to find the good. I like to think that Paula and I share something of the same spirit in that the will to go on was inside us both, guiding us.

Radcliffe's switch to the marathon was probably the defining choice of her life. She blitzed her first professional marathon in London in 2002 becoming the then second fastest in recorded history at 2:18:55.

It was an impressive start and yet, not willing to be second, she proceeded to break the world record just a few months later in Chicago, laying down the gauntlet at 2:17:18.

As a young boy I remember watching her race on television, seeing her repetitive now-famous running nod and lithe slender body. Her pace, even then, I knew was not normal. She said once in an interview that it was never easy for her, that she had to work really hard to get those results. In that admission she was at once infinitely human and yet otherworldly and strong. I was an instant fan.

In 2003 she set the women's marathon world record, winning the London Marathon in 2:15:25. It stood unbroken until 2019.

Like all great stories hers is not without tragedy; she has known the heartache of defeat and injury. She famously dropped out of the Athens marathon with an injury and broke down crying at her body's inability to go on. The British media attacked her then as a quitter and her only recourse to this was to come back fighting and win the New York marathon. The critics stopped talking then.

Bikila gave me heart as a runner, but Paula? Paula gives me strength.

The gods must be crazy

Throughout the countryside, as I run, there are ruins of small cottages and old homes. The simple stone shelters hark back to an older time in the county's past. A time when farmers and animals often lived together, when children died young and life itself could be so raw and cutting. They are the artefacts of my forebears.

Much has changed so quickly. Granny Connell's generation

witnessed the birth of our nation, from the coming of electricity and the automobile to the mobile phone and the Internet.

Modernity has descended on us and made our lives better and we rejoice in it for, as a nation, we endured poverty for centuries. And yet we are also at times confused by it, overpowered by it.

The writer John McGahern said we in rural Ireland lived in a nineteenth-century world until the 1970s. At times we think back fondly to that peasant past in what my father calls the nostalgia of hay. Life was simpler, we all of us laboured together and there was no class system because we were all of us poor.

I have a smartphone now. It is so strange to be so connected to the world in this way. I strove when I returned home to live a life that was a simple one, one of farming and nature and writing a sort of *Walden* of my own, but I too learned that a smartphone can be a great gift, that it can help a man call a vet in the middle of the night, talk to friends on the other side of the globe who would otherwise be lost, and find out the names of stars in the sky.

Every generation now feels as though they are living at the time of total transition. That the world is changing irrevocably, that modernity has come and nothing will ever be the same again, and yet the ceaseless march continues on. Modernity is for ever and while we are at its vanguard at this moment, soon the next generation shall arrive and take up the pick and shovel and continue the diggings and we shall appear as Luddites to them.

When George Edward Dobson, an Edgeworthstown-born anthropologist, sailed up the rivers of the Andaman Islands in 1872 he thought all of modernity was contained in him. That his view of the world was right and that the savages of the Great Andaman tribe he met were a shadow people, a lesser race.

His views to us now seem barbaric and strange but such is the wheel of time.

Dobson, a British army surgeon, was posted to the islands off the coast of India in the 1870s and his writings and photos contain some of the richest descriptions of the Andaman peoples from that time.

The islands themselves hold a pivotal place in the story of man for they are seen as a key stepping-stone in the great coastal migration of the first humans from Africa. It is for this reason that its peoples look African and not Asian.

Its native tribes, including the Jarawa, Onge and Great Andamanese, lived in relative isolation until the late eighteenth century, when the British established a penal colony on South Andaman Island. Named Port Blair, later Port Cornwallis after the brother of the general of Ballinamuck, the settlement would house the political prisoners of India much in the way Australia would hold their Irish counterparts.

Such was the dangerous climate of the penal colony that the Viceroy of India Richard Bourke, the Earl of Mayo, was murdered when he visited there in 1872 by an Afghan inmate, Shere Ali.

The Andamanese tribes themselves were seen to be a vanishing people like the Aboriginals of Tasmania. The overwhelming view of the time was that the superior race of the European was simply replacing them. That Darwin's survival of the fittest was in action.

These were the thoughts of Dobson when he sailed up the river of South Andaman Island to meet with the native people.

The island, he said then, 'was clothed with probably the densest and loftiest forest in the world.'

His presence was announced by two natives and the local chief's wife greeted him. Dobson notes that she quickly put on a government-supplied frock on seeing him to hide her nakedness but soon after, 'perceiving that no ladies were in our boat, she got rid of that unnecessary encumbrance and presented herself in nature's garb, adorned by a single leaf, a garter tied below one knee, and a necklace composed of the finger- and toe-bones of her ancestors.'

The home of the Great Andaman tribe contained two long sheds, containing 110 people of all ages who carried out their everyday activities. He remarked that there was no curiousness about his arrival even when he set up his camera.

On his trip Dobson was to meet a native girl who had been brought up in a colonial orphanage on nearby Ross Island. The mission of the Ross Island orphanage had been to civilise the blacks and train them in the crafts and trades, a practice that had been carried out in other colonial settlements. It was also used as a tool to create 'cut-off people', i.e. to remove them from their culture so as to leave them no option but to become a subject.

The girl who had been brought up from infancy in the orphanage had been given, it seems, permission to return to her people. It is here that Dobson remarks that

This girl I had seen almost every day, sitting in front of the school-house, and on Sunday at church, neatly dressed in white, and her head covered with a fair quantity of black woolly hair . . . [She] was now destitute of clothes, shaved, and greased with a mixture of olive-coloured mud and fat, and married, wanting but the finger- and toe-bone decorations to complete her toilet.

To Dobson the girl proved the unchangeable savage nature of their subjects, in short the backwardness of primitives. To me it is simply a child who wanted to return to her home, a girl who had everything taken from her, trying to find her place in an altered world.

It was a travesty. It was a homecoming.

Dobson would never again venture into the world of anthropology; he became instead a zoologist and worked in the field of bats, becoming a world expert before his untimely death. I wonder now, did he ever reflect on that trip years later in his English home? Think back to the dancing and the welcome, to this real and innocent contact?

Modernity is a cruel and fickle thing, its progress does not mean it is always right. The Andamanese have survived though only number some fifty people from a once thriving community of thousands. Their new masters, the Indian government, have done what they can to help protect their dwindling culture.

I run on past yet another ruin. These houses that litter this landscape are reminders of our biography. I think of the lives that lived in them, of their own sorrows and struggles. That I write, that I think, in the language of the victor, is not lost on me.

We are all of us like that long dead young girl, searching simply for home in an ever-changing universe.

Town mouse and country mouse

I'm a rural man born and bred, and the country life is the life for me. However by times I have had to live and work in cities. Running in the two environments provides two uniquely different experiences.

To run in the countryside is to run in peace; country roads are oft quiet places where one can take in nature and run as it were unencumbered of traffic, time and the business of other people.

Running in cities and urban places provides a whole set of challenges and the urban runner is a smarter runner for they must overcome road signs, marauding cars, monorails, cyclists and fellow navigators of the tarmac.

I do not discount city running, for one can run through

beautiful places, cathedrals of man's genius, for where else can one run by skyscrapers or sports grounds, pass families eating dinner and glimpse domestic lives lived through living room windows.

The urban runner is a runner who must battle distraction, for around every corner lies a new potentiality; a lover, a friend, a coffee date, a business partner.

To run in a city is to see all of man's environment, its joys and despairs, from the wealthy businessman on his way to an important meeting to the homeless beggar striving for his next meal or fix. One can feel elation and fear, love and loss. The urban runner's course through a city is, however, met with possibly our greatest nemesis: the traffic light. The traffic light forces one to stop and wait and in so doing break up a good run into a series of smaller intervals. It can be a great annoyance, when one is enjoying one of the great days, to be forced to stop. The alternative is, of course, to get hit by a car! It is why, I suppose, the parks of every city are so full of the members of our tribe.

Urban running is also harder on one's feet, for the constant whack of concrete and tarmac upon one's legs and joints provides no give and relief. Of all my many injuries in my running life most were caused by urban running.

There are, of course, dangers to country running too: drivers unused to seeing a runner may disrespect them, escaped farm animals may charge, and falls into ravines and ditches while out on trails could well result in broken limbs. It is, however, in country running that I nearly lost my life: running out on a nearby rural road one winter's evening, I set out too late in the day and the fading daylight proved to be a near car accident. Coming by the France Road near my homeplace, a car slowed to avoid me and in the doing a neighbour nearly hit them. The road was utter confusion and much shouting followed, with me the centre of the blame.

'Why are you not wearing a *hi-vis* vest, John?' they shouted.

'I thought I'd be back before the dark hit,' I replied.

'You'll be dead before the night comes.'

I turned for home, tail between my legs. I haven't made the same mistake again.

I'm a country mouse but I could do with some city smarts.

Cliffhanger

I've got a list in my head that I call the book of runs. It's comprised of different runs I've taken around the world in what's turned out to be some of the greatest days of my life. They have often been simple acts of endurance or running by beautiful scenery. What makes them great days is not the place nor even the length of the run but the feeling I have inside me. My run along the Cliffs of Moher was one of them.

Just about a year ago my friend Duncan came to Ireland for a visit. We decided to take a road trip along Ireland's west coast, as I had longed for months to visit the sea after a long winter's season on the farm.

Our drive, along the bays of Galway and Clare, had been peppered with runs by the shore, the sea breeze washing in our hair. We told stories as we ran and joyed in the simple pleasure of being alive and together in that moment.

The Cliffs of Moher are unlike anywhere else in Ireland. Rising 390 feet above the howling Atlantic Ocean, they stand alone, facing out towards the Americas. From them you can see the Aran Islands, the Twelve Pins mountain range in Galway and Loop Head to the south. Situated amidst the ancient Burren landscape, they are one of our cathedrals of nature and receive nearly a million visitors a year.

I can't remember who came up with the idea, but staying in the nearby village of Doolin the night before, Duncan and I hatched a plan to run the length of them.

Duncan is an Australian and that counts for something in a runner because they are a thrill-seeking nation undaunted by pretty much anything. Running by the very edge of a potentially fatal cliff sounded like exactly his cup of tea.

We set off late Sunday morning from the village following a small country road. The landscape is flat and gentle at first, building only slowly and incrementally. Duncan is a fast runner and we kept pace for a while, running alongside one another remarking on the changing limestone landscape, at the nearby farms and the beautiful sea. After the first six kilometres the cliffs started to emerge and my feet started to ache.

It was going to be one of those days, I knew. Things were going to be difficult. I began to slow and Duncan moved onward, facing into the growing winds, his pace unchanged and strong. 'I'll see you on the other side, mate,' he said and took off. I saluted him, giving my blessing, and wished him a good run.

Lumbered now with sore feet, bad runners and on my own, I decided there and then that I wouldn't quit. For no one, I surmised, remembers the day they nearly ran the length of the Cliffs of Moher.

After another few kilometres and some serious hill climbing, I reached a plateau and marvelled at the real cliffs themselves. Tourists littered the grounds, taking pictures and sheltering hats from the gusting winds, but we, we were the only runners. We felt almost superhuman; that this was our track to conquer.

The cliff walk is a beautiful thing, an unguarded trail running right beside the precipice. One has to exercise caution when moving beside it for a wrong step might result in you slipping and falling; it's dangerous, but my God did I not feel alive when I jogged on beside it.

We ran and ran, Duncan moving ceaselessly into the wind, fighting his way south towards St Brigid's Well and Baile Thiar, where the ruins of an old castle lie.

The sun emerged and shone on us as we ran, puffins and gannets called from the depths below while tourist boats bobbed small on the water. I felt in those moments like all of life was here, that in the running I might never stop, that in this space a man could live for ever.

As I reached the castle ruins and the sanctuary of a breather I found Duncan lying in the sun relaxing.

'What took you so long, mate?' he laughed.

'It's my feet,' I confessed. 'I've no support in these runners.'

Duncan slipped the insoles from his own pair and gave them to me. 'These will help, it's 15k back to the car, mate, we've a trip in front of us.'

The run back was beautiful agony, my feet crying out with each step but my soul singing to be there.

The sunlight had already burned my pale skin by the time I reached the descent and saw Duncan move like an old chieftain across the mountainside, wild and free.

The final five kilometres tested me. Limping and sore, I continued on. I couldn't give up, I wouldn't. I had been through suffering and privation before. I had known the darkest night of the soul. This was but another test and walking home would be a crime I couldn't allow. You get to know a lot about yourself on a run. That day I discovered my own sheer ignorance; it carried me for thirty kilometres.

I've not forgotten the pain but above all the memory of the beauty remains. It's there in the book of runs for evermore. It's one of the great days of my life.

Zen and the art of running maintenance

There's something about a straight road that can kill a runner. I'm still on this road and it's focus that's keeping me going.

Straight road running is tough because everything looks the same: the road, the scenery, the cars, the ceaseless litany of yellow and white lines. I realised a long time ago that running was as much about our minds as it was our flesh.

Running teaches discipline and focus. The Finnish long-distance runner and Olympic record-holder Paavo Nurmi said: 'Mind is everything, muscle mere pieces of rubber. All that I am, I am because of my mind.'

Running has helped to make me aware of the present moment and it can be as meditative an act as those monks who kneel for hours. On the face of it I am simply putting one foot in front of the other but there is so much more occurring; one's breathing, one's rhythm, the focus on one's energy.

In today's world, many people find meaning through physical effort, a day becomes good when one has worked out, walked or swum, for the wellspring of goodness is topped up and a feeling of happiness descends upon us. Thoreau himself went for long expansive walks to bring balance to a day. It's a chemical thing, we're told, endorphins fill us with natural happy chemicals and things are good.

But we can also find peace through physical effort. As a farmer I have experienced the same moments of transcendence in cleaning out cow houses as I have in the midst of a long run.

Both have taught me the simple mantra that there is joy in the present moment even though the present moment might be difficult or hard. In a way it has prepared me for just about any situation life can throw at me.

There was a time in the long ago when things were not like this, when I looked to the future. When would my life get better? When would I not feel so bad? When would a lover come back? If it was not the future that occupied my thoughts it was the past and I was stuck in a loop of should have, could have, if I had done this, if I had done that. It was a mental prison that so many of us live in. It was the time before running.

Running long distance requires you to be in the here and now, to be in the immediacy of life. For me, after twenty-five kilometres my mind no longer drifts, it requires my focus because I must will myself to continue on.

The body wants to stop but we realise that we are stronger than the body. Everything starts in the mind, even peace.

We are all of us on the road of life: we might as well try and feel the ground beneath our feet as we move through it.

Turning the corner

Slowly, slightly, I can see the end of this road and the outline of Granard town. It's just as well because I've had to dip into another sports gel pack. My energy is starting to lag and my attention growing weary on this long straight.

Granard is a famous place; travellers know it as a crossroads, a meeting point. It's where we sell our cattle, where one of our famous war heroes met his love and where the shame of a nation was laid bare. It holds a lot of stories.

I take the left turn from the motorway and feel the delight of twists and bends once more. In the distance the looming motte of the town stands high and clear. A worn and broken statue of St Patrick lies atop it and I've often stood there and looked out on the countryside below. On a clear day you can see the province of Ulster from here. It is the land of Heaney, Friel and the rebel Red Hugh O'Neill.

There have been people in this place since our history began and if a town may have a fate then Granard's has been one of conflict.

The coming of the Anglo-Normans to Ireland in 1169 marked the start of eight hundred years of British-Irish relations. It was we who began it all for they were invited by Dermot MacMurrough, the King of Leinster, to help in re-establishing his power base. The leader of the Normans, Strongbow, had in exchange for his help taken Dermot's daughter Aoife's hand in marriage and would, on the old king's death, inherit the throne and lands. So masterful was Strongbow that every child in the country still knows his name eight hundred and fifty years later.

The Normans entered Ireland quickly, establishing a power base as they went. So quick, in fact, that King Henry II visited in 1172 to ensure that Strongbow would not set up his own rival kingdom independent of England. As a bulwark Henry appointed Hugh de Lacy as his man in Ireland to be his eyes and ears and prevent any possible breakaway. De Lacy's lordship in Meath included parts of Longford, then the very edge of Empire and a frontier land between the Anglo-Normans and the Gaelic Irish.

A castle was built in Granard by 1199 on what seems to be the motte and bailey site one can see today. The motte and bailey was to become a hallmark of Anglo-Norman settlement throughout Ireland and the country is now littered with them. Granard's castle was an important staging point for it lay near the border with the sought-after Gaelic kingdom of Breifne (modern day Cavan and Leitrim).

By the time of Hugh's murder in 1186 he had been titled the most powerful man in Ireland and was receiving tributes from Gaelic chieftains and kings in Connaught. He had also fallen out of favour with Henry for marrying the daughter of the King of Connaught without permission.

Such was the importance of Granard as a frontier outpost that the new King John of England, Henry's son, visited in 1210 to help quell another uprising by Anglo-Norman lords. I have tried to imagine this visit and how it must have captured the imagination of the local people. What would they have thought to have a king visit this small place? And I wonder now, do many still know this fact?

King John stayed in the town in mid-August with his large military force. He seized the de Lacy castles and lands in Meath, including Granard Castle, and held them for five years while Walter, the son of Hugh, went into exile.

The area thrived in the next hundred years with profits flowing back to England. Such was the peace and prosperity that English settlers came over to farm the new areas and a small walled town was erected. The walls are now gone, lost for ever; it is a shame, I think, for it could have been like a miniature walled Derry and brought tourists to this place nowadays.

The peace the settlers had enjoyed was broken in 1315 with the arrival of Edward Bruce (brother of the famous Robert) and his three-year campaign to become the High King of Ireland. Edward's claim was a just one, as he could claim Gaelic descent through his mother's family, and the nation had not had a king for some time. His campaign was designed to also create a second front in the Anglo-Scot wars and drain the English of men.

Longford, as a frontier territory, saw much fighting, and Granard, as an English town, was burned to the ground by Bruce's army in November of that year.

It would not be the first time the town was sacked. Bruce's campaign of independence was ultimately defeated in the Battle of Faughart in 1318 in part due to a European-wide famine which killed thousands and weakened his forces. That Edward came so close to a total victory is often forgotten and he would remain for many centuries the only leader to nearly claim the Irish throne and independence.

Breaking from my thoughts, I round the corner and run by the livestock mart and take a look inside. Some jeeps and trailers are already parked, for it is a sale day and men will be coming from around the area with cattle.

I like Granard mart. I've often spent many a good evening here, one meets one's neighbours and friends, catches up on local gossip and generally has an evening out. As a boy I thrilled to hear the older men's stories in the canteen upstairs. Between pots of tea and greasy fries, they talked of times long past. They were some of the first bards I ever knew. They spoke of history as if it had happened only that week, moving from the Boer War to the birth of a new bull calf with ease. Theirs was a world rich with imagery and tales which I only now appreciate in its passing.

We will sell our strong weanling cattle here when they have put on enough weight. Prices are stable at the moment but farming is an unpredictable business. Like writing, one has good and bad years. The leanness of a man's prose output can be a similar reflection to his livestock. It will be a while before we bring the weanlings to the mart, by then too I shall hopefully have finished my writing for the season.

I've written short stories of Granard; it is a different world to me, for as close as it is, they are a different race of people to me. Their view of the world is based around their motte, they look always outward to the stranger. Their world is one of townspeople.

I pick up the pace now as I move past the livestock mart and make my way to the main street. The Catholic church,

St Mary's, stands just before the ancient mound. It too has a place in the story of this town.

Ann

In January 1984, a fifteen-year-old girl called Ann Lovett died giving birth to a baby boy in a grotto to the Virgin Mary beside the motte of Granard.

Ann's passing caused a public outrage; her pregnancy had been hidden from her family and friends for shame and her tragic death sparked a debate about the taboo subjects of teenage pregnancy and pregnancy outside of marriage.

Ireland of the late 80s was a very different place to the one I now run through. The Catholic Church exerted a tremendous pull and power over the people and government and many things we now see as injustices occurred then.

Ann attended Cnoc Mhuire Secondary School at the top of the town. It was the same school my own mother had studied in just years before. Falling pregnant (outside of marriage), as it was known then, was seen as a downfall and scandal and could ruin the reputation of a family. A teenage pregnancy, more often than not, resulted in the girl's being sent to an institutional convent or laundry where the baby would be born, taken from the mother and adopted out. These places were run by various orders of nuns and paid for by the Irish state. They were not places of love or care and many pregnant girls became, in effect, modern slaves, working for the nuns in their laundries, in some instances for years on end. Their babies, too, were not simply adopted but in many cases sold to American families for large money, the profits going to the religious orders.

Recently, a local historian, Catherine Corless, helped to discover the remains of up to eight hundred babies and young children from one such home. They were buried in a septic tank in the town of Tuam, a little over an hour's drive from Longford town. The babies and young children had died, Catherine said, in some cases at a rate of two a day, due in large part to malnutrition and lack of care. The death rate inside that home in the 50s and 60s was five times the national average.

There were many at the time who believed in these institutions, who believed that the Church was carrying out the will of God and that it was for the betterment of the girls that their children born of sin were taken from them.

The language, even the official language, denigrated the children themselves: they were known as illegitimates. It was a system of banal evils, a system like Eichmann's, that was run not by sociopaths but average people who were motivated by personal gain.

It was, however, not devotion that made religious orders sell children, it was not ideology that kept young girls behind eight-foot-high walls. There existed, in this time, many truths in Catholic Ireland. The truth of the clergy who ran things, the truth of the victims who suffered, the truth of the government who oversaw and funded the practices and the truth of the public who knew. All that is concrete and knowable are the remains of the dead, the bodies buried in septic tanks, the fostered and adopted children around the world and the memories of the young mothers, now themselves old women.

This was the climate in which Ann Lovett lived. This was the world in which she died. To her, to confess to her pregnancy would mean the end of her life and the beginning of another.

Ann did what any child would do; she hid, she hid her pregnancy, and told no one, in the hope, perhaps, that it all might go away. Her death on that cold winter's day in 1984 was one of enforced sin, of a world view that had been corrupted by a terrorism of the soul, namely the false power of institutions over people.

She gave birth in front of a statue to the Virgin Mary, I think in the hope that the Holy Mother would help her. She had brought with her scissors to cut the umbilical cord. She was found at 4pm by passing school children on their way home, her little boy already dead, she bleeding badly.

She was brought to the parish priest's house and then driven in the doctor's car to her family home. She was dead before an ambulance arrived.

The people of Granard closed ranks when the nation's media descended on the small town. The nuns who ran the school issued a short statement denying knowledge of the pregnancy, and Ann's family would not speak, and a sort of omertà flowed across the county. The townspeople were portrayed by the media as backward yokels. Recently a solicitor friend talked to me of that time and said we Longford people were as with it as anyone else in the country, that it was a place of modernity too, that we were not the rural innocents, and perhaps I think now they were not yokels but people living in the unfamiliar spotlight of extreme media scrutiny and they did not know what to say to the world.

Ann's death was seen as a tragedy but it was also a catalyst and became another touchstone in the division of Church and state in Ireland. A popular national radio-show host began to read letters sent to the show from women who had also had teenage pregnancies. These letters were to change how Ireland saw itself, how it viewed sex and sin. It was in many ways the beginning of our examination of ourselves and what was being done to vulnerable people in our society.

The folk singer Christy Moore wrote a song about her, 'Everybody Knew, Nobody Said'. A sombre and mournful lament, it finishes with the words:

It was a sad, slow, stupid death for them both
Everybody knew, nobody said.

Had Ann's son lived we might now have been friends for he was born just two years before me. We might have played together, indeed run together. She was a modern Mary and hers, too, was a mournful pietà, carried out for a whole nation to see.

In moving by this solemn place I have often wondered where God was in the time of these institutions, in the time of sinful babies. The acts that were carried out by the religious orders were not in the way of Christ, for he, I know, was a friend of the lowly and dispossessed.

It was a terrorism of the soul; it was a travesty of the Camino. It was Ireland of the 80s.

The difference

Some things happen in living that change the entire course of our lives. Some moments we cannot come back from that remain with us for ever.

Perhaps it is little Ann Lovett that has got me thinking of this, but in a way I've been thinking about it every day for three years.

In a way it is why I began to run, why I still run. But it is not for this moment in my race. Now I must focus for I've many more miles to go.

I will stop for water before I leave the town. I'm thirsty.

Pit stop

I've decided to pull in to get some water before I leave Granard town. I haven't drunk all day and my body is telling me I need hydration. Normally I don't like stopping mid-race but

I've no liquids on me and I don't want to keel over for the sake of prideful ignorance.

I try and move as quickly as I can to buy the bottle of water and get back on course. Stopping mid-race for a total pit stop can be dangerous, for it might just take the will of the run from me and starting up my engine again could become a chore.

I take my bottle and hit the road, drinking as I move. Water is life and all runners know this. I like to think of myself as a camel because like those ships of the desert I can go for a long time without a drink. It's a handy tool to have up my sleeve.

I drink and feel myself easing back into my stride. The water cools me and helps my tired muscles.

Eating and drinking right are an important part of being a runner. If you want to be a good long-distance runner then you have to put healthy food in your body. I tried all sorts of different diets when I started this sport, but in the end I've found a good balanced diet with no processed food, sweets and soft drinks to be the best.

The healthier we become the more our bodies crave healthy food. And in the eating of healthy food we start to take more care of our total wellbeing. I can't remember the last time I was sick and I can't recall having a headache in months. It's not a bad complaint considering where I was just a few years ago.

Now I'm not saying I'm a health freak; I used to smoke and run. But after a time I gradually moved away from cigarettes and I knocked drinking on the head. I replaced old vices with new ones. Going for a long run is as good to me as going for ten pints. It's something my father laughs at but there's a certain joy in waking up after a night of socialising and having a clear head. I'd never go back to the booze, that's what running has done for me.

The water is beginning to work and I'm feeling more alive again. I put on some music to pick up the beat in my heart.

I love Earth, Wind and Fire's song 'September'. It's a great fun American funk hit. It was a number one and I think just about everyone I know loves it.

I sing out the high-pitched chorus and I see some elderly ladies look at me scornfully, but I smile and they smile back and we sort of laugh at my playful buffoonery.

That's the thing I've discovered in running: it is a way to recover innocence. It allows me to be self-delighting, self-affirming and self-deprecating. The road caters for all these different facets of each person. The road doesn't judge us.

I can be a bit of a clown and a scholar here. There's something nice in that.

I drink my water and splash the last of it on my face and chest. I'm feeling a new sense of strength in me. I must go on. I will go on.

The general and the lady

As I turn out the road I pass the Greville Arms Hotel. It's here that another great love affair took place. Before Ann's death, Granard was known as a town of love and leaders. The long

Irish fight for freedom culminated in the War of Independence from 1919 to 1921. It had found its roots in a failed rebellion in Easter 1916 which was brutally suppressed by the British authorities, leading to the summary execution of all its leaders, including one Sir Roger Casement, former exposer of the horrors of the Belgian Congo and the first real modern human rights activist.

Longford was to play a key role in the Irish War of Independence and the leader of the guerrilla war, Michael Collins, was to meet his future fiancée, Kitty Kiernan, here in Granard.

The Kiernans were a well-to-do family owning the local hotel, the Greville Arms, and several other businesses in the area, including a bakery. Kitty met Collins through her sister Maud, who was stepping out with the young military leader's cousin Gearóid O'Sullivan.

Ireland of the 1920s was a brutal and violent place, where death and violence claimed many victims. The Great War of just a few years before had resulted in tens of thousands of Irish dead, many who had fought under the false hope of a granted Home Rule nation.

Kitty's love for Michael has been immortalised in the film *Michael Collins*, which features their first meeting in Granard. Kitty was played by the American actress Julia Roberts (whose Longford accent was something to be remembered for what it wasn't, but we do not mind). Their story is connected in many respects to my own and many other local families, for Collins, as the military commander of the Irish Revolutionary Army, was to be the leader of my own grandfather John. Granddad and his brother Mikey were to join the North Longford Flying Column in the war years and were commanded by local man Sean MacEoin, the blacksmith of Ballinalee, a close friend of Collins.

The county, as a strategic point of Empire, was again to take to the stage as a place of battles and bloodshed. We fought the British to a standstill and treaty negotiations began with Collins himself leading the talks in London. Kitty and he were to share letters each day during this tense time.

One such from just before the negotiations reveals the state of mind of the man and what the country was facing:

Things are rapidly becoming as bad as they can be and the country has before it what may be the worst period yet. A few madmen may do anything. Indeed, they are just getting on the pressure gradually. They go on from cutting a tree to cutting a railway line, then firing at a barrack, then to firing at a lorry and so on. But God knows I do not want to be worrying you with these things.

Collins and Kitty, I imagine, had long talked of marriage and one supposes they had held off until the nation was at peace. Their wedding was announced to occur in November 1922. But the plot of life, as it so cruelly can, was to change their plans. For it was a Longford man who would cause the

Irish Civil War, delaying that wedding for ever. His name: Sir Henry Wilson, the Ballinalee native whose ruined property I have run by.

Wilson had been one of the chief opposers of Irish freedom, and as the leader of British armed forces had shaped policy and military tactics in relation to the British handling of the war. Wilson was assassinated by IRA forces in London shortly after the signing of the Anglo-Irish Treaty. His death caused outrage in Westminster and led to Winston Churchill issuing an ultimatum that Collins sort out the growing problem of anti-treaty forces or British forces would return once more to Ireland.

This ultimatum resulted in an all-out civil war, with Anti-Treaty men, of which my grandfather was one, arguing that a partially free Ireland was not sufficient.

Collins, it appears, took no joy in fighting against his former allies and while en route to his native Cork to sue for peace was ambushed and killed. His death shocked and angered the nation and provided the beginning of the end of the Civil War.

Kitty and Collins never married. Michael was just thirty-one years of age. He had brought the British Empire to its knees but he had lost his life in the process. He was just a few months older than I am now.

Had he lived, Ireland might be a very different place. Perhaps the Northern Irish War might never have happened. We cannot know.

The bar in the Greville Arms is named after him now and its passing trade of customers sometimes stop and take pictures, in this, the town that has known only tears.

McCarthy's Road

I move out of the town, taking a left at the hotel, and pass by the closed Ulster Bank and the local bakery. I place step after step on the road and contemplate its place in this story. I have talked of it much on this journey.

The roads I run upon are ancient things, their old tracks once carried men and beasts. They carried my father in his work, my grandmother as she cycled here for groceries and my grandad and his fellow soldiers in the war.

The road has always held an important place in our psyche. It was to this place we ended up when landlords evicted and burned us out of our cottages, it was here we wandered in the famine, it was here we left this land for evermore to be scattered to the four corners of the earth. Ours was never an empire of earth, it was an empire of the road.

Perhaps it is Granard, perhaps it is talk of the Famine, but Cormac McCarthy's writing has been with me today, haunting each step. In the great hunger, we built roads that led nowhere for food and perhaps, in some way, I feel now my run too is a run to nowhere, but I counter that thought, that doubt that tiredness has bred. It has a meaning and a purpose, it is a jog through history, a run through a wounded landscape pockmarked by invasion and blood and suffering in an effort to understand this place, to understand myself. The road, it occurs to me now, is a place of endless memory and endless time.

The door has been seen as the great device of the Irish stage, for we never knew who would come through it, but the road, the road is where our dramas took place, where the poor old woman, *sean-bhean bhocht*, Kathleen Ni Houlihan walked in search of her four green fields and the men that might return those stolen promises to her. Perhaps out here on these old rebel tracks I shall meet her but today she has the face of a homeless woman, a rent-starved young girl, a drug-addicted junkie, searching still, searching for an Ireland that exists, that perhaps only ever existed in the imagination.

But the road is not just this: it is also a place of hope. It was these same roads that brought our children home, that attracted our people back, that held the promise of new life and beginnings. Every road we walked as a people was the road, in a way, to home. As an emigrant it was these same roads that brought me back to Ireland after years of wandering and I found what I had been looking for after ten years of searching; myself, my sense of who I am.

I may well move over the ghosts of the dead on these ancient things but I carry with me something they did not have. I carry hope.

Toronto

It's been a strange thing but I have always lived in the former provinces of our old masters, from Australia, to Ireland, to Canada and America. I move through these colonial places reflecting on the interconnectedness of history, of the greed of an empire and of the peoples it pushed aside in its wake.

My runs in Toronto were some of the first real runs through history I ever undertook. In the long ago, it seems now, I lived in this city. I ran the same course each time, starting off from my apartment in Charles Street East and running up through the Bloor and Yonge interchange, the city's main thoroughfare.

I would cross then into the Rosedale Ravine parkland and run through its forested alcoves. I was not a great runner then and a few kilometres was all I could manage, and yet each step always brought me a great joy.

In the ravine lands native Aboriginal men sat waiting for drugs or alms or just someone to talk to. It was my first encounter with native Canadian people. They would later become my friends.

Running by the valley road, mighty pines and spruce trees towered over me as cars and trucks passed by. I always cut through the forest at the same point, ending up in St James' Cemetery each time. In the old graveyard lie the tombs of the loyalist families who had fought against the American War of Independence, siding with Cornwallis in the long ago.

There was a tomb I returned to each time, a mausoleum to an old lieutenant who had fought for the British in that war and then again in the 1812 war. His crypt is old and ruinous now, a man and family that came out on the wrong side of history.

I sometimes think of that old crypt, that short run and the life and relationship that didn't work out in that country.

All that remains of that time is memories now. I remember the pines, the loyalist dead and the smile of a girl I once was going to call wife.

A long run brings you to strange places; sometimes it brings you back into yourself. Transporting you to other dimensions and roads not taken.

Take me out to the ball game

Past Pat the Baker's, by O'Callaghans Terrace I see children playing ball in the street. They sing and cheer and it does my heart good.

Sport is something I have come to love. It is a force that brings us together, brings out the heroic in the everyday. In my running I can feel like an Olympian, if just for a moment, by dint of practising the same craft.

Granard has produced its own sports stars but no one quite like Tommy Bond. He's forgotten today, I'd suspect there's not a Longford person knows his name, but he was the first Irishman to play major league baseball in America, a pitcher in the early days of the game. He emigrated to the US with his family in 1862, settling in Brooklyn.

The arrival of the Bonds was in the middle of the US Civil War and one supposes that baseball must have been a distraction for the young man, for thousands of his Gaelic countrymen and perhaps former neighbours were being enlisted, fighting and dying on the battlefields of Shiloh and Antietam. Indeed over 200,000 Irish were to fight on both sides in that war. America has a green history.

Tommy's childhood fancy developed into the making of a talented pitcher and before long he was playing baseball professionally. A member of the Brooklyn Atlantics, baseball's first great team, he excelled, taking a no-hitter into the ninth inning, a feat that few in even the modern game can boast and something that the then eighteen-year-old must have been proud of.

Walt Whitman, the celebrated poet, was a noted fan of the game and had reported on Atlantics games in the years before Bond's debut. Indeed Whitman was to write of the game in his seminal work *Leaves of Grass*.

Whitman saw the sport of baseball as the great institution that could assure democracy in the United States, where men could duke it out on the diamond instead of on the battlefield. It was a sport of the working American and anyone, even an Irish immigrant such as Bond, could become a star.

Bond would go on to play for many teams, including the Boston Red Caps and the Hartford Dark Blues.

He was the first winner of the Triple Crown for his pitching game, a major award, something even Whitman himself would have heard of. There is something amazing in that, in the connection of history, of Whitman and this boy from Granard. In the universe of maybe, perhaps the great poet might have actually watched him or indeed met him. And I wonder now did young Bond know who Whitman was? We shall never know.

Bond's career, like any great sportsman's, went into decline as he aged, and by the 1880s, when the pitching distances changed from forty-five to fifty feet, his number was up. It was said the game changed and Bond did not change with it. By 1881, he was out of the game altogether with a lame arm. He did return to play outfield in later years and eventually ended up playing umpire roles. He died in Boston in 1941 after a lifetime of sports. He was one of the first great players.

Baseball makes me think of Haruki Murakami, the famed Japanese writer. He said it was at a baseball game he knew he would become a writer. It was stories like Bond's that told me I would be an author. It's funny what makes us tick.

Heroes

I've a running hero who isn't a runner, he's not even an athlete, but he's been responsible for some of the greatest Olympians of the last few decades.

Brother Colm O'Connell has been called the Godfather of Kenyan running and with good reason, for he's trained and coached twenty-five world champions and four Olympic gold medallists. It's not bad for a man that came to the Rift Valley in Kenya to teach geography and get away from the cold Irish weather. What's more impressive is he has no formal training in the sport at all.

I first learned about the man a few years ago when I was falling in love with the sport of running and consuming as much material on the subject as I could.

Born in Ireland, Brother Colm joined the priesthood at fourteen, becoming a missionary Patrician brother.

Based in St Patrick's High School in Iten in Kenya, he embraced the Kenyan's natural ability at running and started high-school training camps. Brother Colm credits Peter Foster, brother of 10,000m British Olympian Brendan, for his introduction to the world. The man handed him the training programme and a whistle and that was the start, so the story goes.

It was at St Patrick's High School that Brother Colm was to meet and train Wilson Kipketer, a talented young 800m runner who, under the priest's tutelage and training, would go on to become a world record-holder.

Kipketer was good but Brother Colm's next protégé was even better, David Rudisha. David Rudisha is the greatest 800m runner the world has ever seen. He is the 2012 and 2016 Olympic champion, world champion and world record-holder.

Initially a 400m runner, it was Brother Colm who advised him to pursue the 800m. A member of the Maasai tribe, Rudisha's father is an Olympic silver medallist and his mother was a talented hurdler. David's 2012 London Olympics win is still one of the greatest pieces of running I have ever seen.

From the outset Rudisha took the lead with a blistering pace that his competitors could only follow. His strength pushed all the runners up a gear and into that layer of greatness that only the Olympics can bring out in people.

The first lap's blistering pace was matched by the second as tens of thousands of people shouted and cried out at the thought that they were going to witness something truly special, something unique.

Rudisha's form was a thing of beauty that day. Fast, yes, but even-tempered and measured, he seemed almost calm as he moved around the final lap of the race. He set a new world record that day at a time of 1:40.91. That might not mean much to you until you watch the race and see the pace. There's been nothing quite like it before or since.

Brother O'Connell was back in Kenya, watching the race on television. He never travelled to the Olympics. It shows the confidence he had in his runners that when they left him they were armed for whatever life could throw at them.

I've heard both of them talk since of the good feeling with the ground, that the feeling of the foot striking the ground can be right. That's something I have come to appreciate through my own running, from hard bitter concrete that is not giving to porous dirt roads and spongy indoor tracks. The feeling tells us so much about just how far we can travel in this sport.

As a child I competed in local athletic games barefoot.

I think it was here amongst the other children that I learned of that good feeling in the wet, mucky Irish ground.

Brother O'Connell said that David's Olympic gold gave the athlete immortality. I think it gave it to them both, the priest and the runner, the unlikely duo who conquered the world.

Injury

I'm in trouble. My calf muscle is starting to act up again. I hurt it a few weeks ago and after some physio it seemed to have got better but now, now it's sore and I'm in pain and each step is getting worse.

I'm running down the hill of Granard, out past the school and Kiernan's mills. It's a long easy descending straight. This should be a doddle but it's not.

It's a fact that I've had more injuries in the last few years as a runner than I ever had as an inactive person. Partly, I suppose, that's down to the difference between your early twenties – when you can stay up all night, not get hangovers and run on empty – and your thirties.

I'm not running on empty now, but I am running on pain. It may go, it may pass. Sometimes these things do. As I have said, I have gotten better at stretching, better at taking care of myself, for I am getting just that little bit older, that little bit more delicate, and perhaps that little bit wiser. I am, however, somewhat worried, for though pain is part of life, an injury on a long run can be race-ending.

I don't like quitting, I don't like giving in, and so I'll run on and hope that I can run out this pain, that perhaps it's just a knot.

I've big strong legs, they won't be broken by this assault.

I take out my small bag of nuts and dried fruit. I eat them and try to take my mind off the pain; perhaps my muscles just need some food, perhaps the injury is not back.

Running long distance requires that Orwellian double-think ability. I know I am tired. I know I want to stop, but I also know that I can do this. I know that I can win. I am a universe of contradictions. I am a man with a sore leg. I'll try whatever works to get me home.

The run in the sun

I'm not a stranger to pain. I have been in this land before. I know the difference between long-distance pains and serious injuries and I think this time that it's just a passing jab.

My nuts and dried fruit are gone and I am feeling some-what calmer. My T-shirt is wet with sweat, my music is strong and steady. I've put on the rapper DMX. His loud aggressive beats give me great motivation when the going gets tough. He helped me before. He'll help me again.

Some people go to Spain for a holiday. I went there to run a marathon. It was in 2016 and I can still remember the day and the heat, the sweat and the pain.

★

It had started as a relaxed 10k with my friend Tim. We had been running together each morning for several weeks and our timing and endurance were growing. Sundays were special days where we pushed ourselves to longer feats, 30k, 35k, and on it went until that fateful May Sunday morning.

We set off as we always did at our relaxed pace, talking and joking as we went. At the 10k mark it was agreed we'd go for another round and so pushed onwards; by the 20k mark Tim was tired and excused himself, his day's work done. It was just me then and the race was just with myself. Our track by Talamanca beach and down the port road brought me in contact with tourists and locals. I remember that day another runner, who, moving in the opposite direction, would salute me at each passing. He was a tall thin friendly young man; I owe him a great deal of thanks, for it seemed we kept each other going, each running his own race, each willing the other on to his own success.

At the thirty-kilometre mark I had only one goal in mind: to complete the last twelve kilometres and claim my first marathon. Time was not an issue, time was not a question. It was a matter of just finishing. It needn't be fancy nor fast, just a good jog would do.

The sea helped, for occasionally I would run into it and scoop my hat into the waves and dunk the wet piece of cloth back on my head to cool me. At each passing lap I would welcome its cooling breeze upon my body and wish that the whole race could have been against its shore.

I stripped off as I warmed up, reducing myself to just a hat and shorts, running bare-chested and open, the sweat turning to salt on my lips, face and back.

I had no sunscreen and the rays began to burn me but still I would not stop.

There is something about the last 10k in a marathon that drives one on, that forces one to sink or swim. I passed through so many emotions that day, thoughts of love, loss, life and places that I had been. I saw the past build and fall before my eyes and I saw the future, too, in the land where I was a marathon man.

To this day I know it was love that got me across that line, that made me finish that test. Love of self in a caring way, pride in the ability to just undertake the feat can do so much for a runner. If we don't believe in who we are then how can we ever expect to do the extraordinary?

I finished in the end and carried my limping wounded body into the sea.

The running stranger appeared once more and, seeing me, halted and stranded, came over.

I found then I could not speak for want of thirst and rasped the words: Aqua, marathon.

He smiled, disappeared and returned with a full bottle of water for me.

'Marathon amazing,' he said, to which I agreed and drank. We smiled at one another then, for we did not know enough of each other's language to talk freely and yet we had said all that needed to be. He understood my feat and I understood his kindness.

He clapped me on the back before he left and I smiled and drank and cried a little. I shall never forget that first marathon. The pain was momentary, the memory for ever. I walked home and had a cool shower.

I have been through pain before, today will be no different.

Comeback

I'm making a comeback, the pain in my leg is starting to subside and despite the tiredness I'm not doing too bad. I'm getting towards the wall, I know this and there's no point denying the fact.

The wall is a point in a marathon which every runner hits. Tiredness and exhaustion combine to make the runner want to quit. This is where mental strength comes to play. You have to know you will get through the wall, know that it will pass. Every runner has different ways to get through it, some meditate, some listen to music, others shout and grunt.

I'm not above a good grunt and I've got my go-to phrases to keep me going.

You're a wrecking machine is one of my favourites, followed by a good old-fashioned yell. I fancy myself a Viking at these times, I imagine myself to be the Mountain from *Game of Thrones*, made of steel and brawn, and nothing is going to put me down.

And so, here I am, on a rural Irish road, shouting my head off like a madman, a bearded, long-haired madman, but thankfully I haven't passed anyone; a few car drivers looked at me a bit oddly but that was bound to happen.

I shout and in the act I begin to motivate myself to new lengths.

'I've got this! You can do this! I love you!'

The wall is, as Father Sean would say, a right fecker. I've no more armour left, no energy drinks, no nuts. It's just me, my thoughts and the road.

Clonfin

Pain, doubt and sweat are my bedfellows now as I move towards Clonfin, and yet at the sight of it all worries leave me, for this is a special place. I am running in the footsteps of rebels, in the footsteps of the soldiers of destiny.

At the height of the War of Independence, when the atrocities were occurring daily, the men of Sean MacEoin's North Longford Flying Column stood alone. He was our leader, he was our Arthur.

MacEoin, by virtue of his military cunning, had led to Longford becoming one of the most militarised places in the country. So ingenious was he that he was considered one of the top commanders in the nation. The Clonfin Ambush was revenge for constant attacks by the British. The Clonfin Ambush was a spider's web.

An IED was placed in the centre of the road at Clonfin on a cold February morning. Its aim was to kill as many British army forces as possible, gain weapons and ammunition and strike another blow to the enemy's waning morale.

The landmine was brought to the road in a wheelbarrow by an elderly local neighbour and the men then put it in place. A force of twenty volunteers was positioned near the roadside, and as two armoured British patrol vehicles approached, sometime in the midday the bomb was detonated. A large firefight then followed, with one of the British troops escaping in the chaos, allowing word to be sent to Longford for reinforcements.

But the battle was ended before the additional troops arrived: the IRA fighters flanked the soldiers, killing their commanding officer. The remaining soldiers then surrendered and MacEoin accepted and delivered aid to the wounded.

The victorious rebels took off with rifles and ammunition and made their way through the wild bog land of Clonfin.

The 150 British additional troops, arriving late to the scene, then set about terrorising the area, killing in the process Michael Farrell, an elderly farmer, and severely beating a Clonfin farmer, Thomas Gorman. Gorman would later die from his wounds, the result of a rifle butt to the head, breaking his skull. He was my cousin.

MacEoin's men lay low for the remainder of the month, fearing they would be caught. Moving from safe house to safe house, they evaded capture until the start of March when

MacEoin himself was captured at Mullingar train station. He was put on trial and condemned to death.

A few years ago, my grandmother gave me a picture of my grandfather John. It was the first photo I have ever seen of him, the man I am named after.

He is standing at the Clonfin monument, an old man, lines upon his face, hair thinned. He was, I suppose, retracting his wartime steps.

History does not record that he fought that day in the ambush. Where he was, I do not know, but other men, other neighbours, were there, their sons and grandsons are our neighbours still, for history is all around us and inside us.

I bow my head as I pass the battle site. That British men died here on this remote country road does make me sad. Many had come home from the Great War traumatised by what they had seen; war had made them animals and they could only live in violence and yet were they too not just searching for home? Behind the brutality were they not our estranged brothers?

They were not to find their peace in this life, nor on this bog road. Perhaps in the place where violence is ended, where weapons have ceased, where soldiers become men once again, they could rest. We remember their atrocities and their violence towards us but we forget their own humanity. War is a complicated business. I do not know what else to say.

Failure is necessary

I still remember my first great failure in life. I'd been taking part in local athletic events and performing well, winning local games and medals. I got to like winning. It was a new and nice feeling. I was all of nine or ten. The 100m, the 200m, hurdling and shotput, these were the games I excelled at and with extra training in the local sporting complex in town, I developed a little bit of technique.

It was a week or so before a big tournament when my mother surprised me with my first pair of running spikes. She herself had been a talented sprinter in her youth and took a special joy in seeing me run. I felt invincible in them, like I could fly across the track.

I won the race that week and made it to a provincial event.

The provincials was different. It was an hour or more of a bus journey to get to the venue and once there I saw a lot of new and strange faces in attendance. Children from Dublin and Meath with different accents, big broad-chested boys who could throw the shotput like a man and long-legged girls who cleared hurdles with ease. I felt small and young and out of my depth.

I passed each qualifying race in the 100m comfortably and made it to the finals at the end of the day. The 100m is a special event even in childhood athletics and most other competitors stopped to watch. I naively thought my chances were good; I could see myself holding up the medal and my picture in the local paper back home. It would be glorious. I'd won before, I reasoned, why not today?

The gun went off, we ran like maniacs and I came fourth. The spikes didn't seem so glorious and the image of the picture in the paper quickly faded into a silly fantasy.

It was my first real taste of failure and I haven't forgotten it. There is something heartbreaking in seeing others surge ahead and apart from you in a race, moving at a pace you know you just don't have. Failure is part of running. Failure is a great teacher.

The dream and the reality of running are different things.

We would all of us like to be considered as some great runner, to think that we move as gracefully as a Usain Bolt or a Sonia O'Sullivan, but most of us are just lumbering through, trying our level best to get around the road, the course, indeed to just get out on the track in the first place.

Failure, I know now, is part of life. Without it we would not push ourselves to succeed, to try again, to overcome embarrassment and dismay and put back on those spikes and face the roads (be they metaphorical or real) once more.

As a younger man I was very competitive. Whatever I did I wanted to be the best: the best journalist, the best businessman, the best author, and then when I came to this sport again as an adult, the best runner.

After losing lots of races in recent years I got the message from failure that it was not the winning that mattered, it was the joy of the thing itself. I'm not Paula Radcliffe. I'm not even

Sebastian Coe. I'm just me; a farmer who writes and runs, a man who puts one foot in front of the other each day and finds happiness in it.

Failure teaches us to appreciate the ordinary.

Chamber of reflection

My leg pain has gradually eased. My ankles are getting a little sore now but nothing that I cannot handle. I move past Clonfin at a lane way entrance and I can just make out the horizon line of our hill farm there. The young weanling cattle are fattening on its fresh grass. This was the land of the murdered Thomas Gorman; one day I hope to restore its old house and live and work there. If God is good that shall come to pass and my own yet born children can work and farm it with me.

The future is something one thinks about on a long run and so too the past. I move between the two on this great marathon, for that is what this is. A marathon through my home, through my history, through memory as I know it and as it has been passed down to me.

I round a long bend where my mother cradled the dying victims of a car crash years ago and where I rescued a neighbour's straying cow from being hit by a car. It's strange how she and I can remember this place, this small section of road, so differently. To me an ordinary moment, to her a life-ending one. We are the stuff of memories and this road is a kind of vault.

I run around the corner and pass our old family butcher, simply called Farrell's; his shop is now closed, for the man died of Alzheimer's recently. A few years ago, before his illness started, he told me of how he, too, had been an emigrant and had lived in Los Angeles. He had the job of cleaning the Hollywood sign for a time and told me of sitting up there one evening drinking a beer. I have since told that story to my father who often recounts it fondly. I do not know if Farrell himself remembered that event in those later years.

He was in his last days, beyond memory, a stranger to it, for the disease had stolen the thing that makes us unique. He was, however, one of life's gentlemen and our friend. His funeral made me cry for what had been taken from him. And I think now, as I run by the shop, that perhaps the memory of that Hollywood sign only exists in my mind now and what if I should forget it? What happens to a memory when it is forgotten by all? What does it become?

The Irish are blamed for remembering too much, for recalling every hurt, every conquest, every cruel act of our oppressor, but what is the alternative? We have only our empire of memory, it is the thing that kept us alive and together around the world.

Life is a series of events that we add the narrative to later and recall as past experience, but perhaps memory is more than that, perhaps it is the thing that fuels our very soul.

I shall not forget the butcher nor his stories. I shall not forget the past.

Rest days

Rest days are important when you're a runner. You can't go all day every day; it's just not possible. I like to treat myself on a rest day. I'll take a nice walk or visit somewhere I haven't been before. I had such a day a few weeks ago with my friend Zia Haider Rahman in London.

Zia and I have struck up an unlikely friendship, for he is a well-known author and intellectual and I a farmer from rural Ireland and yet when we are together, we enjoy the simplicity of friendship, the sharing of ideas and a good old-fashioned laugh.

Our walk around London was a tourist day for me, for I did not know his city that well at the time, and so we traversed from Islington to Piccadilly Circus and along the Thames, Zia pointing out famous landmarks and I asking questions to which he had all the answers.

We stopped at the British Museum but left after a deep sense of unease came over us, for the loot of the world, our worlds, was here, from the Elgin Marbles to the Rosetta Stone. There was something inherently sad about that place that I think now reflected on our conversation for the rest of the day.

On some side street, we talked of writing and Zia's new-found fame. Born in a mud hut in Bangladesh, he had immigrated into London, where he lived in a squat.

Zia told me that he had to change his accent because the one thing he had learned early in Britain was that an immigrant's accent would not be treated seriously in this class-conscious country, and so in the evenings he would listen to the BBC news on the radio and educate himself in how to speak. 'This Oxbridge accent gets doors open for you, a South Asian one keeps them closed. One has to fit in and this nation is all about fitting in,' he said.

We walked further through London's Bank district, where he had worked in finance for a time, the grand buildings a hint to the great illustrious past of this city. I countered that he was a celebrated author now, a part of the intelligentsia, that surely these things didn't matter any more.

Zia looked at me then and stopped, saying, 'That was something I never sought, I never sought the fame.'

'Seek or not, you have it now,' I said and clapped him on the back in manly fashion, for I was proud of him.

'But you don't understand, John,' he replied. 'I'm a sort of embarrassment to this country.'

I didn't understand what he meant and told him of all his success, all the awards, the prizes, the fame. They were things I wanted, things I dreamed of. I recounted that there had been a four-page *New Yorker* article on him – surely that must have made him happy.

He shook his head. 'I grew up in squats and council estates, I'm an immigrant, no matter how well I do I'm not one of them.'

I saw only red then and looked my friend in the eye: 'If this were America, you'd have been on *Oprah*. Your life, all you've done.'

Zia shook his head then sadly, for there was something I didn't understand, something I had not seen. He was an Asian man and so would forever be an outsider in Britain.

'I'm an oddity here,' he said. 'In America it's different.'

That I was white and he was not was something I stupidly hadn't considered, that my road was made easier was a truth that he had not said, for I had not thought it. We were both children of Empire but both our roads were very different for the faces we wore. It made me embarrassed and then angry at the world we lived in, in the society we called home.

Later, when we took the tube back, Zia asked me what it would be like to be a person without morals. What would your world be like? I think now that world was there in the halls and monuments of that former superpower, in the statues to the dead white men, in the colonialism of the mind that existed and still exists, no matter how far one rises.

We came home late and had some warm milk and went to our beds. It was a rest day I have not forgotten.

Keep on keeping on

I have been running for the last three hours or more; I am no longer sure. Time has vanished, time is beyond me; I know only running now. At this point, I no longer need to think about the act itself, my legs believe that things will be this way for ever and, good legs that they are, they have agreed to this new routine and oblige me.

I can feel a small amount of lactic acid building up in my shoulder but I know, too, that that will leave me. My lungs are strong and calm. They are the part of me that is most fit, they have become my compass, they guide everything else.

I am approaching the final stage of this journey. Another ten or so kilometres and I shall be done. Perhaps it is more? Perhaps it is less. I can no longer tell. A part of me wonders if a runner's high shall emerge at any time. I could do with that last shot of energy, but perhaps today will not be one of those days.

Runner's high, I'm told, is a rush of endorphins released after a good run, it fills the runner with a sense of elation and goodness and is the body's way of helping us push through the pain barrier. It is a wonderful feeling, a feeling of oneness. But there is no sign of it today.

I run on, pain follows me in every step and a small voice calls me gently now, it snides that I should just quit, walk for a moment it says, but then my conscience reasons we are still a long way from home; the quickest way to get there is to keep running.

It is a matter of mental work now, a matter of outwitting myself.

Between my feet and this journey rests my mind. I'll run with it.

The nature of language

I am shouting my mantras more frequently now. I call out in English and Irish. I urge myself on in the old language because there are times when I just can't find the right word.

Different things come to us when we are running. Of late, lines of poetry keep descending on me. As I neared Granard motte I thought of Kavanagh's 'Shancoduff' and his elegy to the poet's life. At the Clonfin Ambush site Heaney was there digging for peace. Perhaps running is a poetry of its own, a sort of language or space where the mind becomes open to this art, open to finding new meanings and rhythms.

A few months ago, I discovered the writings of the poet John Clare and have been attracted to him ever since. In him I found a kindred spirit, a brother of the land.

Born in 1793, in the village of Helpston near Peterborough, he became a farm labourer as a child. His poetry was born from trouble, with his first collection, *Poems Descriptive of Rural Life and Scenery*, published in order to prevent the eviction of his family from their cottage. The work was an immediate success and he was hailed as a voice of the working class.

Through him I have learned that it is OK to talk of the local and in the doing one can find a sense of the universal. That all of life is as much here as it is in some city's high street.

His poetry, so beautiful and delicate, reflected a natural world that is my own experience and yet in him I see the fear in all men who undertake this life, that they shall not make a living, that they shall succumb to the dangers of drink and demons, that we, too, shall fall, as John Clare did, into madness and poverty and death.

I worry about this writing life, this life I live. Farming, running, they are real and tangible, and yet I do not know what to make of this craft, this writing business, for I am, after all, only just one man and all the world is a big place.

My mother says I have a gift and that it is a shame not to use what has been given us. God, she says, gives us all pearls. My brother was given his hands to make things; I was given the word. I worry about the word but perhaps that is the thing that keeps me on my toes, that keeps me digging.

I push the thought out of my mind. Clare's fall will not be mine. I have already been to that place. I already have known that darkness. It's why, I suppose, I'm here on this road today.

All nature has a feeling. All runners know doubt. All writers have fear.

I still haven't found what I'm looking for

The road has broadened out again. It is wide and breathable. Cars move by quickly but I feel a new sense of horizon about me. I feel somehow that I am in the big skies of America again, cresting along its great roads, inhabiting its frontiers.

A few years ago I spent an evening in Joshua Tree in California. I was working in Palm Springs, shooting a documentary, and realised the famous national park was near me. With a few dollars, a beat-up truck and the music of U2, I made my pilgrimage to that hallowed land. I'll never forget driving out to the desert, seeing the trees and mountains as far as I could behold and the feeling of the magic of the American outdoors. I finished that drive sitting atop the truck's bonnet, staring at unfiltered starlight, sipping on a can of beer and smoking a cigarette, and in that perfect moment I promised I would return.

It took me four years. Much happened in the intervening time; indeed, there is something about returning to a place that is unchanged to see how much you yourself have grown. I found in Joshua Tree a new reflection of myself.

The day had been hot, far too hot to run, with temperatures of 100 degrees Fahrenheit. I had passed the time until the allotted hour in a nearby second-hand bookstore outside the town of Twentynine Palms and leafed through its many editions. In my rummaging I discovered a signed edition of Frank McCourt's *Angela's Ashes* for a dollar and began talking with a soldier from the nearby Marine base on the epic march of Napoleon to Russia. A communications officer, he told me of his life on the base and how he hoped there would be no more American wars in the Middle East, for he was a peace-loving man.

In the evening, as the sun was sinking and the day cooled at last, I left my camp ground at Indian Cove along the park's northern edge. Running cross-country I set out through the desert scrub. I carried only myself, a worn LA Dodgers hat and a selection of music to suit the mood. I had long dreamed of my return here, to breathe in the air and escape the congestion of the city of Los Angeles.

I had been practising my running in downtown LA for many weeks in the build-up to this day, setting off each morning from my digs in the arts district then on to Skid Row and through Chinatown, finishing each day in Elysian Park. In the long ago, the Elysian Fields were the place through which the dead entered paradise for ever. It was from here I trained for my great desert trek, for my run through this valley of my old life.

There are times, I think, when we become the actors in our own dramas, transforming into our cinematic selves. Joshua Tree was my Ben Hur, my Lawrence of Arabia, my own promised land.

Cutting out through the sands of the Mojave Desert which rule this section of the park, I witnessed the valley come alive with feeding animals; rabbits darted before me as birds and hawks swirled high above in search of passing lizards.

The Mojave is a special place where bare rocks break through the soil, making one think of sleeping giants waiting to arise and shake the land. The Joshua trees watch the land silently as living monuments to this magical space.

Following no trail but my own, I used the huge monolithic rocks dotted through this area as my landmarks. I moved out across the sands for miles, turning at last for home as the sun dropped behind the nearby mountains of the Morongo Valley.

Returning to my campsite, a coyote stood before me in the setting sun, wild and free. I slowed to a stop and we stared at each other for a moment before he turned and slowly walked away to his home.

This was one of the great days, the great moments in the book of me. They form the memories I shall reflect on in years to come when I am old on my farm in rural Ireland. They shall tell me that I was lucky to see the world. They are the moments from which runners are made.

Runs such as this embolden us, nourish us, they keep the fire in our bellies when we are again faced with a winter treadmill or an injury. It was as good to me as a penthouse apartment in any great city, for I was in the cathedral of nature, something concrete shall never match.

It was joy as Pheidippides spoke of. It was what life is all about.

I finished and played air guitar to U2's 'Lemon', dancing on the spot. I looked like a right fool. But that's OK.

The blacksmith

I'm nearing Ballinalee again. I'm closing in on the great loop I have undertaken. To my left stands the old blacksmith's forge of Sean MacEoin, our hero. Restored, reshaped, its fires have not blown in nearly a hundred years. It is a quiet reminder of another time, a reminder that war changes all things, converts tradesmen to soldiers and farmers to mercenaries.

The gun in Irish politics has been a factor in our lives for hundreds of years but the gun itself is British; it is not a physical thing, rather a cache of wrong choices or, in another phrase, right decisions that were *not* taken by its elite.

Pacifism had been attempted in modern Ireland for decades, from Charles Stewart Parnell to John Redmond. Irish politicians had asked British politicians for the right to be allowed to peacefully rule themselves. Thirty-five thousand Irish men had died in World War One under the impression that their sacrifice would lead to that self-government. We had asked another country for the control of our own affairs (with self-imposed limitations) but we would not leave our old master wholly, we would still be part of Empire and loyal subjects.

The choices that were not taken by the British then, in the failure to grant Home Rule, led thus to the limitation of peaceful solutions and the drift towards violent ones. The choice or unwillingness to make the right choices by Britain then can be seen as tragic when viewed from the long view of history.

Those tragic choices begat political certainties that we all live with to this day.

That MacEoin was to become a rebel was unknown. That he was good at killing was not a choice, rather a fact that he discovered. I do not say that men did not exhilarate in killing, for surely some did, but what began as the decisions of Empire turned into what the writer and director Neil Jordan called 'the unstoppable movement of people towards a concept.'

As the Yankee would say: You put a rat in a corner, he will fight to get out.

MacEoin's war began with the Irish Volunteers and later the North Longford Flying Column, a unit of the Irish Republican Army, long before the events of the Clonfin Ambush in 1921. After many smaller raids in the local area of which he was the leader, he came to national prominence with the assassination of RIC Inspector Philip St John Howlett Kelleher in the Greville Arms Hotel in Granard on 31 October 1920. I do not think he knew then all that would befall the area, all the violence and death that would follow.

That his home of Ballinalee would come under attack was an unforeseen event. The sacking of Granard a few days later by British troops was the direct result of that assassination and its burning unopposed had, one supposes, emboldened the enemy.

They sought then to continue their reign of terror that same night by destroying Ballinalee and in so doing to end the threat of MacEoin and his men for ever. It's said the sky glowed orange from the flames of the destroyed town of Granard.

To MacEoin, Ballinalee represented a last stand. If the village fell his column would have no base and the rebellion in the midlands of Ireland would be over. That Cornwallis had ridden through here and hung the fallen men of 1798 must have played on the volunteers' minds. Could history repeat itself?

Troops were stationed at each crossroads, the roads over which I have run today, in the hope that a flanking movement might be made by his men before, outnumbered, they would be overrun and gunned down.

The British Black and Tan troops numbered with a large force; armed with machine guns, trucks and heavy artillery they faced the small brigade of the North Longford Flying Column with the Killoe regiment waiting in the wings.

The fight began at nightfall when the troops entered the village. MacEoin ordered a surrender to which gunfire responded. The volunteers threw grenades into the British side which were returned with machine-gun fire upon MacEoin's command centre, Rose Cottage.

The night was pitch dark, with only the muzzle flashes of gunfire lighting up the black. In the darkness there was confusion, so much so that the British troops fired upon their own fellows.

At a lull in the fighting, MacEoin called on the troops to surrender for the second time, to which they once again re-engaged. He insisted then that the fight would be to the end.

Outnumbered and outgunned, they fought until 5am when the British fled the scene, bringing their dead with them.

MacEoin later recalled that:

We held our positions and the coming daylight revealed a remarkable scene. About the area in which the lorries had been drawn up were pools of blood, and strewn all over

it were items of military equipment, revolvers, thousands
of rounds of .303 ammunition. There were also boxes of
chocolates, boxes of boot polish and every conceivable
commodity, all of which had been looted from shops in
Granard.

It was the only village to not fall in the entire war. It was
their Little Big Horn, he was our Sitting Bull.

Neighbours past

I run on by Donal Hughes' house. A gentle soul, he lived here
with his mother until his premature death a few years ago. I
still remember that morning, for I was on my way to see the
cattle in Clonfin and a melee of cars were gathered at his front
gate. I knew then, I cannot say why, that he was dead. He had
been sick with the bug, as it is called here; the cancer moved
quickly through him, claiming yet another neighbour as it had
done my uncle just weeks before.

His land is run by other men now and his mother went
to the Manor Nursing Home in Edgeworthstown soon after.
I passed her once there before she, too, died but she did not
know me.

I had heard for several days after his death she set the
table absentmindedly for the two of them, forgetting his
departure.

The house stands now as a reminder of the greatness of

normal lives, a testament that we are all of us but moving through this world. It is as important as MacEoin's forge in its celebration of the ordinary bounty.

The Berlin Wall

I've hit the wall. I'm broken. I'm not human. I can't go on. There's nothing right in this place and why in God's name am I doing this?

The run, the journey, the whole thing is madness, a sort of crazed madness. I'm tired. I'm worn out. My legs hurt. My feet hurt. My shoulder is sore. I've no water. I've no gels. I've no help and I've run out of songs to listen to.

I've hit the wall and nothing will be the same in this run any more. No one ever said marathon-running would be easy. No one ever said marathon-running would be fun. Each wall is different and this one is a bitch.

That little voice of doubt isn't so small now and it's roaring and complaining at me. By times it takes the form of my father in his puzzlement at my undertaking, at my very sport. It turns then to my mother, wondering why it is I run so far all the time. As I reach the top of Ballinalee hill it turns to visions of laughter, times when I was made the fool in school, in life. I'm a sort of jester, a stupid clown, a Don Quixote, but at least he did battle with something.

This is not a wall: it's so much more than that, it's a quest against myself.

With each step now, I'm in agony and I want to stop but the stubborn man that I am won't let me.

As I pass the Thomas Ashe community hall, I think for a moment I know something of the hunger striker's journey. But then dismiss the thought as an insult to the man.

I run by the school and face down the hill, gravity with me, thinking that the descent will give me newfound wings, but that too is a foolish hope.

Hitting the wall is a result of running out of gas, or to be more precise the body's sugars and carbohydrates are exhausted and the body begins to slowly shut down. There are only a few options when it strikes.

1. *Stop.*

   I really want to stop. Every fibre of me wants to just stop, sit down, lie down and quit. Stopping would be the easiest thing in the world. I just need to quit moving my feet.

2. *Get a gel or drink into me.*

   I've no food left. I've no water. I'm a camel without a hump and though the village shops are close I've no money left. That was another foolish move on my part. I could ask them for a drink, I know all the shopkeepers and there would be no problem, but there's a part of me too that doesn't want to stop for fuel as it will feel like a sort of quitting. A giving in, and I don't want to do that.

3. *Distract yourself.*
This is the third and final choice. I focus on something else other than the tiredness and pain. I think about nature, or I count clouds or I listen to a podcast. Some running books even suggest doing your grocery shopping in your head as a way to get through this. I shall choose this route.

I've broken through the wall before. It's never some Herculean moment where one does battle with some mythical beast, rather it's a sort of slinking, weak surmounting that isn't sexy or heroic; it is just an act of survival. Like the images of the East Berliners scrambling through the rows and rows of Russian razor wire. They do eventually get through but they're badly torn in the process and come out tattered and dilapidated.

The voice won't shut up. I know this voice. We have a history. It tried to break me three years ago. It tried to kill me. A darkness had taken me then and drove me towards self-slaughter. It was in another season, another time, when I was not a runner, when all joy and hope had been taken from me.

I call it the Lost Time. I was stuck in a bedroom for six months, unable to leave, for melancholia had taken me. The Lost Time took everything from me, a love, a life, a marriage.

To have a life reduced to just four walls is a sentence I shall never commit again.

I remember now why it is I run. For all this long day I have not addressed that fact.

I run so that I might never go back there. Never go back to that place, to that time. Running came to me, as I said, as an idea, a stroke of inspiration on how to remake my life, how to become a whole man.

I once heard the preacher of an Australian homeless shelter say that salvation comes through the feet. I have lived that line each and every day. The thief, the voice, did not take me then, and it shall not take me today. The Lost Time. The Lost Years are over.

It was Liam my actor friend who first ran with me in those days. We had neither fancy runners nor training clothes, he was in an old Limp Bizkit hoodie from our childhood and I in a stuffy jacket and sweatpants. Over local roads and forests we moved. He pointed a way towards that elusive thing called joy and the promise of what life could be again. Oh, how often I asked him would life return to normality and he assured me that things would get better, saying our mantra: 'It's all over and it's all about to begin.'

I, we, took those first runs to escape the Lost Years, but in the doing, I found a strength I never knew I had. And my runs with Liam transformed from an escape to a destination.

I don't run from the Lost Times any more: I run for them. I run to bring joy into my heart. For in every step I know that

I am alive and here and in this present moment. I move as a Buddha, a disciple. I move as a man in love with life. In love with the soul of the world.

I run because in this act I prove my living, in every step I prove my strength.

This wall as the wall of darkness is but a temporary thing, a passing shadow. Like the murmuration of those starlings, a memory of times past made visible if only for a second. I am not that boy any more. I do not know that man any more.

My life ended in that room in the Lost Time but it also began again.

Every time I hit the wall, I undergo this journey, and each time I am reborn. Today will be no different.

I save my greatest mantra for last and I tell myself I am proud of me for coming so far, for really the race was never just this marathon, it was so much more. I think of all those who love me: my family, my girlfriend, my friends and neighbours.

I listen to Van Morrison's 'Jackie Wilson Said' and smile. I look to the sky, grunt and roar. I'm a soldier of destiny. I'm a rebel. I'm a runner.

Heroes

The world of running is not without tragedy. From Steve Pre-fontaine to Abebe Bikila, there have been athletes who have suffered more off the track than on it. Indeed the road would seem in some strange way to have been the only place where they could find solace, where they might truly be alive.

I first discovered John Akii-Bua a few years ago. He appeared out of an accident, a stumbled-upon article that soon developed into a fascination with the man and his short-lived career. I think of him today as I run, of his own trials and sadness, and see that we are all of us in this together.

Born in Uganda in 1949, he first came to the notice of athletic officials as a teenager. Talented from the start, it was under British coach Malcolm Arnold that he made the switch to the 400m and found his athletic calling.

Hurdling is a sport I greatly admire for in it is not just speed but great technique. The hurdlers must use their mind and their body in unison in order to clear each jump. The hurdler must also have a small amount of luck with them, for even the greatest can fall in this mad dash for the finish.

The 1972 Munich Olympic Games are now remembered for the horrendous terror attack and murder of eleven innocent Israeli athletes by Black September. But it was also the place of Akii-Bua's world-record-breaking run. For 47.82 seconds he held the world's breath, beating Olympic champions and claiming his place in the pantheon of greatness.

History does not remember that glorious moment, instead it seems shrouded in the bloodshed of those terrorist events, making other endeavours appear insignificant.

Perhaps it was here that Akii-Bua caught the disease of tragedy, for upon his return to his native Uganda his own drama began. It was a short and brutal thing, punctuated with sadness, loss and delirium.

Promoted by dictator Idi Amin as an example of the best that the nation could be, he was given a house whilst simultaneously purges began on his tribal group the Langi. He was to lose friends, family and neighbours at the hands of Amin's death squads and was powerless to act or speak out for fear of his own life.

Undeterred or perhaps driven by his own death, he continued to train, placing again at the 1976 Montreal Olympics in what would be the defence of his title.

The 1976 Olympics was also to be a showdown with his closest rival, Edwin Moses of the US. Moses was the only man the world record-holder feared and the race itself would be one of the highlights of the games.

Tragedy was to strike once more, for Uganda boycotted those games, forcing Akii-Bua to watch as Moses took the gold that should have been his.

As political violence increased in his home and a war with nearby Tanzania in full flight Akii-Bua sought refuge in neighbouring Kenya, where he lived in a refugee camp with his family before finally being rescued by the Puma sporting company who transported him to safety in Germany.

A broken man, he returned to the 1980 Olympics but failed to place, his training and prowess wasted by the purges and intervening war years. His fall from greatness was the final victory of tragedy.

Akii-Bua was to die, aged forty-seven, a widower, his record broken, his greatness a forgotten memory.

One wonders, can a life revolve around a single moment, a single minute – John Akii-Bua's centre rests on that track in Munich in 1972. Is a gold medal enough to keep a man from tragedy, to keep a man alive? The track, that ground, seemed to be the only place where he could truly live for ever in happiness. All the rest was loss.

I leap now not for joy but in memory of a great runner and all that could have been. He is, to me, an Olympian of the heart. We are tied together in our tragedies. He too runs beside me today.

The Big Smoke

Dublin is a flat city and a great place to run. I lived in the Big Smoke last year for a time, working on a radio chat show when the farm work was quiet. The job had long hours, the pay wasn't great and I had to rise at 4am to get to work, but it had one great perk: I finished just after lunch each day and had the sunny summer evenings all to myself. Ireland in summer is when the country comes alive, for it does not get dark until nine or ten at night and people live whole second days after they clock off.

My first great run around the place was and is my favourite of those few months, for it brought home to me the very nature of this nation, the interconnectedness of the place, that the entire country operates as some giant parish where you could equally run into Bono on Dame Street and likewise meet your cousin by O'Connell Bridge. Though I had swapped the country lanes of home for concrete pavement, I never once felt alienated, such is the *meitheal* of the nation.

It was July and the day was warm when I set off from my digs near the Grand Canal on Dublin's south side. Running west towards the city centre, I passed through the city's Georgian district, where row upon row of beautiful red-bricked houses sit. It was here that Robert Emmet, the doomed rebel, once resided.

Emmet is a name remembered by all not for his failed one-day rebellion which led to fifty dead rebels after a storming of Dublin Castle in 1803, but rather his infamous speech from the dock during his trial, in which he said:

> *Let no man write my epitaph: for as no man who knows my motives dare now vindicate them, let not prejudice or ignorance asperse them. Let them and me repose in obscurity and peace, and my tomb remain uninscribed, until other times, and other men, can do justice to my character; when my country takes her place among the nations of the earth, then, and not till then, let my epitaph be written. I have done.*

Emmet was to be hanged and then beheaded for his uprising.

Running in that city was a new experience for me then, for the excursions were filled with foreign sights and sounds, buskers sang through the air at St Stephen's Green while pedestrians chatted on their mobile phones. Where once I would have to contend with tractors on country lanes, I found myself being stopped and started by pedestrian lights, running through seas of people, catching overheard bits of stories, dodging pigeons and swooping seagulls, by food vendors, restaurants and donut shops. Running in the city was a feast for all the senses, exposing me to new and different experiences. In place of cattle and horses, I found cyclists and scooters, and the din, always the din, of traffic, beeping, ebbing and flowing, and I thought myself a sort of Whitman, wandering through this cityscape, seeing it for the first time.

At the Gaiety Theatre I'd peer in to see some famous stage actor or playwright drinking in the bar or meeting in the foyer, its walk of stars bearing the handprints of the great Irish actors of the stage. I'd run on through the city streets, making my way to Christ Church Cathedral, and pass down to the River Liffey before taking a left along the quays and heading out to Heuston Station.

The Liffey is the lifeblood of Dublin city, the place where the Viking settlers first arrived, the site of the gunboat which bombed the Four Courts in the Civil War and where the famous Guinness barrels were ferried to the port to be shipped around the world.

As I ran along the quays to the train station, rows and rows of cars passed me by with commuters leaving the city. They beeped and flashed, exclaimed and cursed, for theirs is a life of slavery to the road. I do not envy them their journey, to drive each day for hours to get to homes in the midlands only to repeat it all again the next morning. I served my time as a commuter and there is no surer way to break a man.

At Heuston Station I paused to look at the road for home, for Longford, for even in my days in Dublin I longed for my weekends in nature to escape the city. I turned and crossed the bridge, and following on the opposite side of the river from here, I had ample view of St. James Gate, the home of the Guinness brewery. As a young student I lived here for a summer working as a security guard and in the evening, when the brewing would be done, the vats and exhausts would exude the vapour of malting barley through the city, creating a smell that no other place can claim.

The city has grown and changed in the last twenty years, for the Celtic Tiger, our economic wonder, created tower blocks and fancy offices. I watched them as I passed and wondered just who works there.

The concrete ended and a small wooden gangway appeared on the river side and I moved past junkies and homeless men admiring the view. We do not have such people in the countryside and it hurts my heart.

During that time in Dublin I spent a day at a shelter recording a radio programme on homelessness and I recognised some of the faces. They waved and nodded to me as I ran and

I answered them and we were as equals in that moment, our struggles forgot; they are in so many ways the *daoine le Dia*, the people of God, for theirs is a world so much closer to the divine than we shall ever know, their suffering, their heart and their bravery exposed for all the world to see.

'I'm out for a run but I'll see you again,' I shouted to one of the younger men I recognised from the shelter.

'That'll do, pal, enjoy the spin.'

I passed Bachelors Walk, where a massacre occurred in 1914, when British soldiers opened fire on an unsuspecting crowd. It's a fashionable area today, the blood long washed away. At O'Connell Street Bridge I waved to the statue of Daniel O'Connell, the Emancipator. From here I could see the General Post Office where the rebels of Easter 1916 put up their last fight, from where our proclamation was first read, the bullet holes still visible on its mighty stone columns. History is never far from one in Dublin.

Under Pearse Street station I heard a shout and turned and it was a girl I had not seen in years. 'Arra, John,' she said, and it was my primary school classmate returning from work. 'You're out running?' she said.

'I am,' I laughed, and I stopped and we talked of old times. I wrote a short story about her father a year ago, for he has become a good friend, and she thanked me for the words. She works in banking and is rarely home any more. Dublin is her home now, she says. It's not the countryside but it has what she needs.

We embraced and I told her I'd see her again and that hopefully it won't be another ten years.

By Nichol's Undertakers I moved and walked in the footsteps of Leopold Bloom. It is as much his city as it is mine and together now we continue our odyssey through its streets. The Jew and the running farmer, we sound like a bad joke and perhaps Joyce might have liked that.

I cut up past the Natural History Museum and the back of Trinity College; Sam Beckett attended there, I remarked, and as I glance to the ground, street plaques tell me that the Wildes of Oscar fame lived near here and literary Dublin had come alive in just a few roads. Surrounded by my heroes.

Turning left past the Taoiseach's (Prime Minister's) offices, I headed for home. Hilary, my friend, had put me up and was cooking dinner. A falconer and arts journalist, he was training a small hawk in his house. She eats chicks and is partial to hunting wood-pigeons. I'd yet to see her fly but perhaps this evening, in the good weather, we may go out with her Hilary remarks.

An opera singer trains in his conservatory and I can hear him through my digs' window.

Hilary tells me the best nights are when he tackles 'Ave Maria'. 'It would make you cry,' he said

I sat and listened to the man and felt a calm come over me, like the balm of a creator spirit, the sweat from my run drying on my face.

There is no place like Dublin: you never know what you might encounter in this, the parish at the centre of the world.

Living in a coded land

I run down the hill and on towards the village centre of Balli-nalee. I am wounded but I am not broken. I have refocused my mind, refocused my efforts. I am part road now, part moving thing. The lactic acid in my shoulder has dissipated and I've found new life in me. From where it comes I do not know.

I am slow but I am here. At the village crossroads I pass the statue to our blacksmith and the bench to our war dead. Granny was supposed to open that memorial a few weeks ago. As the last surviving widow of the War of Independence she held a special place in the hearts of all the locals. Her death was a final link with the past, broken.

A bronze Sean MacEoin looks towards Longford town in the distance. Dressed in his military uniform he watches all who pass through this coded land. I see once again Cairn Hill, the timepiece of our lives. It's said the murderer of an ancient Celtic queen is buried upon its brow. From here we can view our lost green field of Ulster, shrouded as it were in misunderstanding.

I do not know what MacEoin would make of this nation now, of what he fought for. The village has changed in a hundred years. We cling, in ways, to our past in an attempt to understand this present. This modern world that has come rushing in on top of us, battering us in new ways with unseen problems.

The old battles are forgotten and new layers of history have come to make their layers upon our souls.

That MacEoin would have died for this place is true, for after the Battle of Ballinalee and the Clonfin Ambush he was captured and sentenced to death by the British High Command.

Labelled as little more than a murderer, he wrote a letter to his childhood friend Father Jim Sheridan, saying:

Dear Jim, Last week I was tried, convicted and sentenced to die three weeks from today. My poor mother was here yesterday to request that my body be turned over to her for Christian burial. They refused and told her that my body would be buried in quicklime in the prison yard. If you write immediately, I will receive your letter before I died. Farewell, Jim. Pray for my soul.

His misspelling of the word die perhaps indicates the fear he felt; his would be a martyr's death and yet it was not without a human toll.

He was released at the last moment as part of the Anglo-Irish Treaty negotiations and his spared life helped form the new-found state.

Here our paths diverge, for my family did not support the Treaty and pushed on for a full reunified Ireland. There are wounds from the Civil War that exist to this day across the nation and things that are still not said.

That MacEoin is loved and disliked by some still shows the

bitterness of that war and that history can never truly die, for it is still happening daily.

The British threatened to return if the Civil War was not ended and this fact must have weighed heavy on MacEoin's mind. It is said that more lives were lost in the one year of the Civil War than in the entire struggle for independence and many terrible atrocities occurred on both sides. In the end there were no winners and the fight which we had exalted, exalted nothing, only tragedy and bitter resentment that have lasted until recent times.

The Church sided with the Free State troops and denounced the guerrilla fighters, saying that those who took part in war were guilty of grievous sins and could never receive absolution.

I do not know everything that happened at the time; that death haunted the entire country is true, that friend faced friend and, indeed, that MacEoin carried out a pacification in the west and brought the rebel men under control of the free state gun, are facts. That my grandfather was on the opposite side does not escape me either. There was much running then too but they were runs of a different kind, runs towards dreams of a nation that could never be. We do not talk of the Civil War any more, and perhaps there is a comfort in that silence.

I feel only sorrow now, and a low anger that the Empire itself, through its unwillingness to grant a full freedom, turned brother against brother.

The sweetness that all men longed for night and day, as Yeats wrote, never came for these men, not for MacEoin nor my grandfather, not in this coded land where blood begat blood. We defeated one enemy only to find new foes in ourselves.

MacEoin left the army a few short years after the war ended, changed for ever by what had happened then. There were men, I'm told, who never spoke a word to him again for his actions in that time. In this place even our heroes have weight upon them.

I reach out and run my hands upon his bronze back, living history embodied in us both. I run on for Longford, for Soran, for home.

The Navajo

We are not alone in this post-colonial landscape, we have never been. It was on a run in America's heart of Arizona that I came face to face with a leader of the Navajo Native Americans and found something of ourselves reflected back.

I had come to the Navajo reservation to run, for it is a sacred act here.

The Navajo nation is a big place, as big as Ireland; it is a land of milk and honey where beautiful desert plains give way to rolling grasslands. It is a special land.

It stands alone as one of the few tribal nations to regain its homeland during the American wars of conquest. Why it was that they and not, say, the Apache or the Sioux returned home is not so clear for all the great tribes fought as bravely as each other.

The history of the American inland empire was founded on a lie, for its core principle of 'Manifest Destiny' was the fiction of a newspaper editor. This destiny enshrined the right given by God to 'overspread and possess the whole of the North American continent'. It was this credo that allowed for the 'great experiment of liberty' to occur: namely the wars of conquest on the ever-expanding frontier.

So successful was the ideology of 'Manifest Destiny' that we can see it shape the Nazis' *Lebensraum* theory some sixty years later. In both, we see morally justified colonialism; in short, the act of dispossession devoid of guilt.

That the Irish, too, took part in this experiment is not lost on me, for we were part of that great ride west. There was excitement in it for the people who went, but tragedy for the people who already lived there.

Monument Valley is a sort of mecca in the nation. A temple of nature with its cathedral of vast monolithic rocks rushing through the red desert soil, it is a religious and sacred space. My run was, I suppose, a pilgrimage to the Old West, to the West of the imagination, and yet it became a Camino in the way of Thoreau's transcendentalism, for the creator's hand was everywhere visible in this place.

Having camped under the desert stars the night before, I set off at 6am, before the heat of the day could break me. The run was twenty-seven long miles and the winds of the Arizona and Utah plains swept the red sands as I descended into the park. They call this place Tsé Bii' Ndzisgaii, the Valley of the Rocks. It is a place that draws men to it, a place of magnetism that cannot be explained. In the quiet of the morning I ran alone by stabled horses and soaring eagles high above.

The Navajo legends of this place concern their own foundation story, of their movement into the fourth world, and how gods and monster met here. They simply refer to themselves as the 'Dine', the people, and all actions, even those of long ago, happen under Father Sky and Mother Earth.

It is the same sky under which the Navajo began their Long Walk of 1864. Hunted by the US Colonel Kit Carson, a noted Indian-killer, the tribe were, after a brave resistance, rounded up and forced to walk a 500km journey to a detention camp in New Mexico. Many died on the walk and more still in the camp.

As I ran I thought of that march and the fear that must have been in the hearts of the Navajo in that eighteen-day journey. It had been said to me that it was heartbreak that killed many on their sad trail, a fear that they would never again see their homes. In their trek I see, too, my own people's forced migration to this continent. As the Navajo battled waring US colonels, we fled our shores in the coffin ships of the Atlantic, bound for the harbours of New York to escape Famine.

As I rounded the Rain God Mesa I thought how vacant this valley would be without its people, how the songs of this place very nearly died and what then would become of the sacred?

At the twenty-mile mark I began to loop around the great earthen road and turned back for the campsite. The sun was still rising and the heat of the day had not taken me yet. I was thirsty but that was my only complaint.

I breathed in the clean air and saw a jack rabbit break from the brush and vanish into the horizon.

In the Navajo tradition, running creates a living cord between earth and heaven, it is a means of communication between the living, the dead and the holy. I felt something of that as I passed through the scrubland and saw the landscape waken for the day; it was pristine and beautiful, a red oasis of serenity free of tourists at this hour.

After four years in the detention camps of Bosque Redondo in New Mexico and at great cost to the Americans, the Navajo began negotiations with the US government and together General Sherman and Barboncito, their great leader, agreed to the return of the Dine to their four sacred mountains.

It was not all of their once-vast nation but it was one of the few victories of native people in this country.

Hot and weary, I saw the road for the camp and a wind blew and cooled me. It was the breath of the creator and I welcomed it. I ate breakfast in the shadows of the monoliths and packed my bags to meet a fellow runner, the Navajo Vice-President Jonathan Nez.

At Window Rock, the seat of the Navajo government, we talked of the past and present. Dressed in cowboy attire, with short hair and turquoise amulets, he has the face of the modern Native American with all the problems of modernity crashing in upon his people.

He noted that I was Irish and that I would know something of the Navajo people's experience, to which I agreed.

I asked him then of the Long Walk and how it had affected his people. He told me that it was in the long ago and that his people were blessed to return to their homelands.

'Not many tribal communities could say they came home after being rounded up,' he said. 'They had resilience and that never-giving-up blood that flowed through them flows through us,' he added.

We talked then of history and how nations can leave it in the past. He looked at me and talked of the land, that most powerful of things to the Navajo. 'We need to let our lands heal . . . it should be at the forefront of our discussions . . . we are its stewards and we are supposed to be protecting our land . . . there's a lot of scars here and we really need to let those wounds heal.'

I countered then that the scars were those of colonialism from the US government and big business. He told me that colonialism hadn't ended for there was a new form, capitalism. 'It is engulfing us,' he said simply.

There was a sadness in that room, but it was not mine, nor was it the Vice-President's; rather it was as John Moriarty, the philosopher and mystic, said, 'the sadness of the place'. On the Vice-President's soul weighed the souls of 500,000 Navajo people and the mantle of leadership with which he was placed to bring these people through the new colonialism and all its challenges.

We talked of running for a time and shared our love of the act. He had recently run a marathon through his home and expounded on the beauty of the place. Monument Valley is a good run, he told me, to which I agreed.

I was not the first Irishman to come to this place nor indeed the first member of my family, for twenty years ago a young priest and distant relative Father Francis Gray had been stationed here for a time. Upon leaving the Vice-President, I drove to Crownpoint Mission, following an old letter of his.

On the path of objective chance I came to meet Sister Maureen, who remembered him, and together we drank ice water and she read his letter.

The Navahos don't seem to have an innate desire to master nature. This comes from an inherited caution and respect. Like the ancient Celts they lavish their skills and endless patience into works of art – weaving, jewellery making, pottery.

The landscape is wild and free, mostly desert with red and blue rocky mountains and little groups of houses here and there vanishing into the landscape – not standing out against it. It is the Indian Way to want to pass through life without disturbing anything. The spirit of the earth, air and water are to be respected and the land and all it bears are treated with consideration.

Corn the fruit of the land is sacred to the Navahos.
They use it like holy water. In the morning at prayer,
a devout Navajo holds a pinch of it in his hand, when
finished praying he sprinkles it on his path, puts a little
pinch of it on the top of his head for good luck and tastes
it for good harmony.

Sister Maureen then showed me the church and I asked her if she thought it strange that I had come.

'There is a beaten path to Crownpoint. I've been here for thirty-five years and I know that everyone comes here for a reason. Sometimes people come into our lives and we don't know why and sometimes we never do,' she said. 'But I think you know why you are here?'

'There is a reason for everything,' I replied, and told her of my work into the study of colonisation, and how we Irish were not so different to the Navajo but that things had changed for the better for us, that modernity had improved our lives and not those of the Navajo, not yet.

In the small church she showed me their altar built from the stones of the four sacred mountains that have defined the lives of the people: Mount Taylor, Hesperus Peak, San Francisco Peak and Blanca Peak. Each of the stones was selected by the local priest and a local medicine man.

We prayed then for a short moment and Sister Maureen asked me about my meeting with the Vice-President.

'He is battling history,' I said.

'He is right. You can't be a prisoner to your past,' she said. 'There are people here who still talk about the Long Walk but the world has changed since then and you must keep going or it will move by you. We must all of us keep moving.'

In the church there are three icons: the Apache Christ, the Navajo Madonna and Blessed Kateri Tekakwitha, the first Native American saint. By the icon of the Apache Christ reads the question: Can Modern Christians go beyond inherited stereotypes and find the sacred where they do not expect it?

As I stood there and reflected on my journey that day I felt I had an answer of sorts to that, for the sacred is within and around us. In the Navajo, in the nun, in my runs around the globe and the glory of the dispossessed. For Christ, it seems, came for us peoples, the other peoples, the people of time and history who have remained despite suffering and death. We are all of us one.

Father Frank finished his letter with the statement: 'In journeying to a distant world one can see one's own world more clearly.'

It was not until I left that place and came to run in my home that I understood what he truly meant.

Home stretch

I'm on the Longford road now and at the bridge of Ballinalee I shall return to my *tír*, my land. I see the trees my father has planted in the bog growing strong and upright. They shall outlive us all.

When one closes in on a marathon, strange things happen. The sense of ending comes upon one, it is both an ease and a regret. In a world beyond tiredness, we move, struggling onward as weary men with a feeling that our souls have earned our rest, our break, our supper.

I pass Granny's lane and round the long slow bend by my family home. I think they shall be wondering where I have been all day, for I told them I was simply going for a run and what, what shall they make of my story?

This stretch of road holds no great history, only the story of my family and our neighbours. I remember them now as deeply as the great deeds of the rebels and poets of the last few hours.

In that front field we burned the whin bushes to clear the land, by the bog we played as children in the rushes, listening to the cries of curlews and sky goats.

In the fields our cows graze happily, this year's calves by their side. We made hay in them years ago but the weather has changed now and hay is a seldom thing.

At the river side the neighbours and I made rafts each summer to the delight of old Mickey Doherty the local senator; here too we fished its streams for trout. This is all the world I know and the one I remember best.

I want to stop now and walk the last part of my run but I have a little more length left in me and a little more miles to go. I will finish soon, I tell myself, and think of the laughs and jeers that Mam and Dad will make when I tell them what I did.

I have been an emigrant for ten years, I have lived around the world, but it is this place that has always called me back. These fields, these cows, these roads. It is the place where I feel alive. Today I have been a migrant through this land.

I'll run on if just a little more. I aim for Killoe now, the lovers' parish. There's just a short more ways to go.

Pride and Prejudice

Killoe is called the lovers' parish, for it was here that Jane Austen's one true love did live. The Lefroys and their ancient walled manor are all but gone from this place, yet their greatest son lives for ever in the famed author's pages. I know this story well, for I wrote a book about the real-life man some years ago. Thomas Lefroy, the Chief Justice of Ireland, the man of law and order, was not always so; once he was a boy in love with a girl.

Born in Limerick in 1776, the young Thomas came from a well-born but poor Anglo-ascendancy family. Bright and energetic, he was championed by an uncle and sent to London to study in Lincoln's Inn for the bar.

It was while in England he was introduced to a young Jane Austen through a family relation and thus began their courtship. It was a brief but powerful thing that changed them both for ever.

Little evidence of this time survives but Austen makes clear reference to the young Lefroy in her surviving letters, mentioning his gentlemanly character, good looks and pleasant demeanour. They attended several dances together and it seems that their affections were mutual.

Their relationship has since been immortalised in the film *Becoming Jane* where actor James McAvoy inhabited the brooding young man torn between love and obligation to his family. That they fell for one another, as the film suggests, is indeed true, for on Tom's departure from England on 14 January 1796 Jane wrote:

> *At length the day is come on which I am to flirt my last with Tom Lefroy, and when you receive this it will be over. My tears flow as I write at the melancholy idea.*

Thomas could never be with Jane, for he was expected to marry for wealth and move up the social ladder; love, true love, with Jane could never be for she had neither of those things.

Whether Lefroy became the basis for Mr Darcy has long been debated and yet their character seems of the one kind. Their adherence to class structure points most clearly to Jane and Tom's affair. Darcy, however, gave to Austen what Tom could never do. She righted the errors of her own life in fiction, granting herself the ending that she had longed for.

They would never meet again, with Lefroy marrying soon

after to a well-doweried lass, thus fulfilling his family's wishes. Of Lefroy's feelings we know little, but in old age he did confess to having been in love with her and on learning of her death travelled to England to attend her funeral. Theirs was a first and lasting love.

Having married well and moved up in the world, Lefroy was to take over Carriglass Manor here in Killoe, building its present grand house. Now a member of the Anglo elite of the nation, he controlled a vast estate of tenants and workers. Indeed members of my own family worked and lived here.

Lefroy himself would change from that brooding, love-struck man of his youth when he became the Chief Justice of Ireland. He was responsible for the exportation of countless people to penal colonies; his is a conflicted story. As the years progressed his intransigence and uncaring attitudes would become well known; an anti-Semite and anti-Gael, he bitterly opposed Catholic Emancipation and forcibly led his tenants to vote along Tory and Unionist lines.

His most famous trial, of Young Irelander John Mitchel, would make headlines around the Empire, with the political prisoner being sentenced by a packed jury to hard labour in both Bermuda and later Van Diemen's Land, then the toughest jail colony in the world.

Mitchel was eventually to escape and make his way to America, becoming in the process one of the most famous public figures of his day.

It is, however, the quieter history of Lefroy that is

remembered here, of his unwillingness to help in the Famine and his rack-renting, anti-Semitism and rotten-borough practices.

The manor, perhaps fittingly, has fallen to ruin. It stands as an elegy now, unoccupied, haunting the landscape, a spectre of another time. Our colonial history slowly crumbles in this place, fading out like a bloodstain on cloth, as a ghost against the morning light.

Both British and Irish, he is part of our story for good or bad, Mr Darcy or no.

On the shortness of life

I run past our neighbours' houses nodding and waving as I go. One asks how I'm doing today.

'Tired' is all I can say. It is all I can muster. I have not spoken in several hours and it is strange to hear my voice.

By my brother's house I look to see if he is home, but with no van in sight I surmise that he is at the factory, working. He has been a great friend to me through everything; I joke that I'll get him out running some day. I was his shadow as a child, for it was he who built our rafts for the river all those years ago. His talented hands were evident even then. He, like my father, has taught me so much.

At Doherty's Cross I turn right and follow the road to Esker. Mary Anne, our neighbour, is looking at her cattle. She is a gifted horse-breeder and better farmer than many men of the area. She chides me that her stories are no longer safe, for I may write them down one day.

I struggle on. The end is coming and it is just ignorance that keeps me focused now. Running a marathon can feel like climbing some huge mountain, some Everest. There are peaks and plateaus, valleys and troughs, and the journey, though less dangerous, is as real to me.

I look towards Cairn Hill and think that it must have been the first real climb that our neighbour Paul Devaney knew. A mountaineer and explorer, he has climbed six of the seven highest peaks in the world. He has attempted to climb Everest twice but both times has had to turn back. He will, I think, try one last time.

I find in him a kindred spirit who understands what Seneca wrote so well, that it is not that we have a short time to live but that we waste a lot of it. I shall not, on my death bed, reflect that I squandered a day on this earth. The Lost Years gave me something that I have come to be thankful for: they gave me the appreciation of time and the want to use it well.

We have been granted the princely wealth of life and it is ours to spend how we see fit. The words of my grandmother and a long-dead Roman philosopher echo together, thousands of years apart, with the same message: it is a small part of life in which we really live, so live it well.

The finish line is nearly in sight now.

The road as Salvation

In a gallery recently I saw the Saudi artist Abdulnasser Gharem's piece *Siraat*. It depicts an image of a road with the word *siraat* painted upon it over and over again. The word itself translates as path; its meaning is doubly so, for it is both a straight road and the road to paradise.

I wonder now, can the same road be and indeed point to the salvation of ourselves from our history?

It was these roads that brought the Empire to us, these roads on which history was made and blood spilt; these spaces I have passed have brought sad stories to my ears. It would seem this whole long day I have recounted and relieved the

wounds of that past, searching for answers like a man with a broken heart.

We cannot undo the marks of Empire. I cannot undo the fact that I now speak and think in English, nor that part of this nation is still not united with itself. I cannot today change that Aboriginal men were hunted for their heads nor that Native Americans were driven from their lands. I cannot change these things but I can remember them and, in a way, pay respect to them by not forgetting.

This history is both Irish and British, one not to be forgotten and one that can't be remembered. That Britain does not recall all its crimes which were our suffering forces us, all of us post-colonial people, to look to ourselves for solace, to look to ourselves for peace. That has not been an easy journey, for after Empire ended we saw only those who had belonged and those who had betrayed.

We were not simply victims in this nation: Irish people took part in its expansion and prospered. They played their role in its dramas; it is not so simple as good or bad. As deplorable as the actions of, for example, Henry Wilson were in the Boer War and Burma, he prided himself on being a good man, he was not without feeling. Even close to his own death he helped in the petition for clemency for Sean MacEoin, a sworn enemy. Wilson, Cornwallis, Lefroy were not evil: they did what they thought was right. It is only now, in the long shadow of history, that they have come out on the wrong side.

That members of my society, or Australian or Anglo-American society, benefited under Empire is true, that they helped shape its course is beyond doubt. Are we simply now to label them as tyrants?

It is not a comfortable thing for us to remember and indeed it has brought me sadness today, but it has made me think, as Faulkner said, that the past is not over, it's not even past.

We are a part of Empire and it is a part of us, be it British, Aboriginal, Navajo, Burmese or Irish.

Like the disciples seeing the wounds of Christ after Easter we must make peace with our scars. This landscape heals us as I know their own lands do for others. We must be as the murmuration, seeing the soul of the world for what it is, our history washing over us, enriching us, no longer a place of hurt, like the wings of the starlings bringing beauty and tenderness, making us ultimately better people.

Walk don't crawl

My road is at an end, my marathon finished. I slow this great steam engine to a halt and walk now for the first time in many hours. I am tired. I am worn. I am a different man to when I started.

My road has not been an easy one but it is the only road I know.

I take a seat by the quiet roadside amongst the grass and wildflowers and let the days light wash over me. I listen to

'Clair de Lune' on my headphones and crush the bud of a buttercup in my hand, letting the yellow colour stain me. There is such beauty in this place. I am elated and alive and there is a joy in all the small things under heaven.

I stretch out my weary legs and ease my muscles gently. I softly knead my calves and take off my runners and massage my feet. They are pale and white in the bright day. A small blood blister has grown on my right foot but I do not mind.

I want to tell Vivian of my feat and call Mam for a lift home, but instead I sit here and watch the world go by, if only for the briefest moment.

It is a beautiful day and I am happy. As the song finishes I breathe in the passing birdsong.

I stand up and decide I'll walk home. Home to the animals and fields that know my name.

Acknowledgements

This book would not have been possible without the help of my friends and family. I wish to thank my father, who from my earliest days regaled me with the history of our home and our nation and to whom this work would not be possible without. To my grandmothers, who though they are departed remain within these pages. To Zia and Lily, my dear friends; Stephen Rea for friendship and chats; Ross Laurence for a place to write, groomsman duties and for showing me around LA. To my mother and extended family for their continued support. A special word of thanks to the people of the Navajo for allowing me to visit their nation and for taking the time to speak to me about their history. To Hilary White, Bob Barton, Duncan Graham, Liam Heslin, Father Frank Gray and all those who have run with me around the world. A special word of thanks to Sonia O'Sullivan, a hero who has become a friend. To all my readers who have come with me on the journey from *The Cow Book* to this book.

Understanding murmurations was made possible by the excellent journalists at *WIRED* magazine, where I discovered the notion of murmurations and phase transitions.

A special word of thanks to my agent Marianne Gunn O'Connor who believed in the book, and for Antony Farrell at The Liliputt Press who was the first to champion it. To Kris

Doyle, my editor at Picador, who believed in the book and for his wonderful editing and guidance. To Frank Greally for his help in understanding the world of running, and to Davy and Cormac for their work on bringing this book to a wider audience. To Mary Reynolds, our one-woman force in the county, and Father Sean Casey and the people of Longford who have all shaped this book and helped me explore our shared history. To the writings of Doctor George Sheehan who showed me running could be talked about in a book.

Last but not least, to Vivian, my wife, who read every word of the book as it emerged. Thank you for everything as always.